America's True Heroes

To Jesse—

America's True Heroes
Stories of American Veterans

Nicholas Rider

Island Time Publishing

Monroe, Washington

America's True Heroes
Stories of American Veterans

by Nicholas Rider

Published by:
Island Time Publishing
P.O. Box 488
Monroe, Washington 98272
U.S.A.

Copyright © 2006 by Nicholas Rider

Third Printing

Library of Congress Control Number: 2006922857

Printed in the United States of America

ISBN 978-0-9788182-4-1

This book is dedicated to my Grandpa, John Haney, who is my inspiration, best friend and a Marine; and to my Grandma, June Haney, for all her love and support.

Contents

Introduction

It is my pleasure to present this book as a form of appreciation to our veterans of America. The freedoms we enjoy today are the work of the people who have strived, struggled, suffered and sometimes died for what we have here in America. We should never forget or take for granted their gift to us.

My hope is that the accounts in this book will help us all become more aware, thoughtful and understanding towards our veterans and those in active duty.

I began this project at age 11; by gathering autographs of the veterans I met. After having many very interesting conversations, I learned of the incredible sacrifices each one had made for our country and felt it was important to record their stories of valor. This is when I began compiling their stories in book form. I gathered these true-life stories over a two-year period. I tried to keep their accounts as much in their own words and styles as possible.

I sincerely thank all who are in this book, who generously gave me their time and confidence and for their many encouraging words. Thanks also to those who sent me names and introduced me to more veterans.

Nicholas Rider
2006

JAMES R. ADAMS

Branch of Service:
    U.S. Army (AAF)   WWII
    U.S. Air Force   Korean War
Years of Service:
    Active Duty and Reserve 1942 - 1956
Outfit:
    15th AF, 459th BG, 756 Squadron
    Training Command-
    98 B Wing, 342 Squadron
Areas Stationed:
    U.S., Italy, Japan
Aircraft:
    B-24, B-29, B-17, AT-7, AT-11
Specialty:
    Navigator, Navigator Instructor, Training Aids
    Officer

During WWII, Mr. Adams graduated from Mather Field, California and was sent to Davis-Monthan AFB in Tucson, Arizona, where his group trained in gunnery, and then to Westover Field, Massachusetts for their final phase training. They were given a new B-24 made by Ford Motor Company. Mr. Adams was assigned as navigator. His group traveled to North Africa by way of South America. His plane was using too much gas on the way down to Brazil to make the leg to Dakar. They removed four men and baggage and were told they could make it. They continued on and arrived safely. They flew missions in Tunis, (Northern Africa), until Giulia

Field in Italy was finished. Eight percent of their flying personnel were lost on the way over.

On their 15th mission to Austria, their plane was badly damaged over the target. It was no longer possible to keep up with the group. A 109 finished them off over Yugoslavia. They were fortunate to catch a sneak spy plane back to Italy. Mr. Adams ended the war as an Instructor and Training Aid Officer.

During the Korean War, Mr. Adams' reserve commission had expired by a year and a half. The President re-installed the commission and Mr. Adams was called back in 1951. He was given refresher courses in navigation at Ellington Field in Houston, Texas and then sent to Randolph AFB, Texas to be assigned to a crew. Next to Lake Charles, Louisiana for Phase training, and finally, Travis Air Force Base, California to be assigned a B-29 fresh out of mothballs. The destination was Naha, Okinawa. Their station was Yakata Air Base, Japan. During this time, they flew some 28 combat missions, all at night.

"I was just a plain Dogface, trying to get the job done and get home. The only thrill I had in a mission was when my feet hit the ground. Out of the crew I went overseas with in WWII, only the bombardier and I made it home, the rest blew up about a week later in Romania. The crew I went down with were on their first mission and I had just seen them at the briefing earlier that morning. When we hit the ground due to a flooding rain, a tree, and a rock pile, I had to be carried everywhere. I was just a burden to all. But due to the grace of God and the kindness of total strangers, I am here today."

ANONYMOUS

Branch of Service:
    U.S. Air Force
Years of Service:
    1943 - 1946 WWII
Outfit:
    8th Air Force, 379th Bomb Group
Areas Stationed:
    Kimboltan Air Base
Aircraft:
    B-17
Specialty:
    Waist Gunner

"I had a unique situation. I was born in Seattle, Washington in 1926. My Mother took my brother, sister and myself to England for schooling. Because of the war, our schooling was interrupted and we had to work in an aircraft plant, join the Home Guard, Wardens and Firefighters. When the Germans bombed our plant, we did not have guns for shooting down aircraft or any other way to defend ourselves. The only thing we had to protect the plant was sticks (Cricket stumps). When the Americans sent us all kinds of guns (including machine guns), we were finally able to defend ourselves. The Germans could have taken England after Dunkirk without a problem.

I joined the American Army in London, at the age of 18. The real heroes during the war were all the pilots that flew the fighter planes from 1938 to 1943. This is because, when the Americans first came over, they flew to their targets without fighter escort. When we flew missions, we always

3

had fighter planes flying with us. When we bombed Berlin, the fighters could not fly that far with us, but would always escort us back to England.

We always made it back to base. For the number of sorties we flew, we lost many good friends. We would return to the barracks and find a lot of beds not occupied.

I am sorry I do not want to say anymore. It is an experience I hope you will never have to go through. When I returned to civilian life, I decided to leave my war experience behind. I lost a lot of good friends."

HAROLD ARENDT, Jr.

Branch of Service:
>U.S. Army (Corporal)

Years of Service:
>5 years service: Cold War 1948 - 1949
>>Korean War 1951

Outfit:
>1st Cavalry Division, 13th Signal Corps,
>>Photographic Unit

Areas Stationed:
>Fort Ord, California; Fort Monmouth, New Jersey;
>Fort Lewis, Washington; Camp Lawton, Washington

Specialty:
>U.S. Army Combat News Photographer

"My unit camped out in pup tents as we fought our way north in Korea. My job was to accompany the infantry as we took enemy held hills. I filmed our troops as we attacked the enemy. I also filmed the Greek, British, and Thailand troops that were attached to the 1st Cavalry Division. I filmed our artillery, tank, and other military units. We had two photographers in my Division. We each had our own jeep and usually a driver who protected us when we were under fire by the enemy. I was wounded by enemy Communist artillery fire and lost most of my hearing while accompanying a tank unit of seventeen Sherman tanks as we crossed the DMZ into mountain positions. I received the Purple Heart and the Greek Gold Medal for Bravery.

I attended the 1st Cavalry Division Commanding General's morning briefing and filmed General Matthew

Ridgeway (who replaced General Mac Arthur as Supreme Commander of the Far East Command) as well as General James Van Fleet who commanded all United Nations troops in Korea. I filmed for the American Red Cross and did a secret assignment with our Ranger Forces."

WM. LEE BAUGH

Branch of Service:
    U.S. Army (Major)
Years of Service:
    1968 - 1988
Outfit:
    55th Aviation Company (VIP)
    2d Student & Faculty Battalion
    281st Assault Helicopter Company
    29th Transportation Company
    Headquarters Battery, 3rd Battalion
        (Hawk)
    Service Company, Berlin Brigade
    NATO/SHAPE Support Group
    S1, 43rd Support Group
    Commander-382nd Transportation
        Detachment, 43rd Support Group
    27th Transportation Battalion
    Division Support Command, 4th Infantry Division
Areas Stationed:
    Republic of South Korea (1968 - 1969); Fort Eustis,
    VA (1969 - 1970); Republic of Vietnam (1970 - 1971);
    Echterdingen, Federal Republic of Germany (1971 -
    1973); Homestead Air Force Base, FL (1973 - 1976);
    West Berlin, Federal Republic of Germany (1976 -
    1977); Belgium (1977 - 1979); St. Leo College, FL
    (1979 - 1981); Fort Carson, CO (1981 - 1983);
    Republic of Honduras (1983 - 1984); Bremerhaven,
    Federal Republic of Germany (1984 - 1986); Fort
    Carson, CO (1986 - 1988)

7

Aircraft and Trains:
    OH-23D; UH-IC; UH-1D Helicopters
    U.S. Army passenger, freight and special command
    Diesel trains
Specialty:
    Flight Engineer/Line Chief; Instructor/
    Administration Assistant; Assistant Platoon
    Sergeant; Motor Officer/Executive Officer;
    Senior Train Commander; Personnel Officer;
    Training Officer/Assistant Operations and
    Intelligence Officer; Joint Movement Control
    Officer; Chief, Movement Control Team; Plans
    and Intelligence Officer

As the Flight Engineer/Line Chief in South Korea, Mr. Baugh was responsible for the maintenance and flight safety of individually assigned light observation OH-23D helicopters. He participated in numerous missions in support of visiting dignitaries from various foreign countries to include the President of the United States, his cabinet and staff. He was also responsible for supervision of maintenance and flight safety of four additional light observation helicopters and five troop/cargo helicopters.

As an instructor/Administrative Assistant at Fort Eustis, Mr. Baugh was responsible for preparing lesson plans and instruction of students on the maintenance procedures and applications for various models of helicopters. He was the Administrative Assistant to the Commander of the Helicopter Maintenance Training Division.

In Vietnam, Mr. Baugh was an Assistant Platoon Sergeant/Flight Engineer. His responsibilities included the daily assignment of combat, enlisted crews for eight-assault attack, UH-IC helicopters, including himself as one of the crew assigned. He participated in sustained aerial flight, in support of combat ground forces. He further participated in over 250-hours of aerial combat missions over hostile territory in support of operations against communist aggression. He preformed all duties and functions required of a combat leader in support of those personnel assigned directly under his supervision. In addition, he was personally responsible for the maintenance and safety of flight of individually assigned attack helicopter and supervisory responsibility of the remaining seven attack helicopters assigned the platoon.

In Echterdingen, Germany, Mr. Baugh served as Flight Engineer/Administrative Assistant. He was responsible for maintenance and flight safety of individually assigned troop/cargo UH-1D helicopters in support of VIP missions throughout the Federal Republic of Germany. He was Administrative Assistant to both the Company and Battalion Commanders.

As Motor Officer, he was responsible for the operation of a consolidated motor pool performing daily maintenance on over 163 tactical vehicles and trailers belonging to a Hawk Air Defense Battalion. He also provided vehicle support for interservice headquarters within an Air Defense Brigade and intraservice agencies collocated with the command. His major additional duty as Executive Officer of a Headquarters Battery, in support of CONUS Air Defense, was the Strategic Forces deployment and special Presidential Support missions.

During the time Mr. Baugh spent in West Berlin as Senior Train Commander, he commanded U.S. Army passenger, freight, and special command diesel trains transiting the Soviet controlled German Democratic Republic. He was responsible for processing all required documentation with

Soviet Army Officers at the Marienborn Checkpoint.

In Belgium, as Company Commander, Mr. Baugh supervised and executed the training, discipline, and supply needs of 259 assigned personnel. He administered to the housing needs and morale of an international troop billet occupied by several separate units.

On January 1, 1981, Mr. Baugh graduated "Magna cum Laude" from St. Leo College, Florida in Human Resource Administration.

As an S1, Personnel and Administration Officer in Colorado, his accountability was as the primary personnel manager for a 2,000-person support group. He managed the development, motivation, and proper use of personnel. He acquired and screened officers for key positions. He was also the Group Commander's principle writer.

Next, in Fort Carson, CO, Mr. Baugh was the Training Officer for a 1,800-person support group comprised of an Engineer Battalion (combat heavy); a composite combat service support battalion and seven attached units. He was responsible for development of long-range training plans, to include administering Army Readiness Training Evaluations and Skill Qualifications Test. He was also responsible for the training of Reserve Component Units hosted by the 43rd Support Group. He served as the Operations/Intelligence Officer in his absence.

In Honduras, Mr. Baugh planned, supervised and implemented the movement and transportation requirements for a Joint Exercise in Central America. He prioritized transportation allocations for maximum effectiveness. He directly coordinated utilization of land, sea, and air vehicles. Mr. Baugh directly contributed to the humanitarian aid of the Honduran people; planned new roads to deliver food and supplies to indigent areas;

established airstrips and airlifted supplies and medicines to the Honduran people. Mr. Baugh was commended for detailed planning ability, which reduced redeployment costs, by 4.3 million dollars.

During his time in Bremerhaven, Germany, Mr. Baugh supervised and trained twenty-six personnel, including German nationals, in coordinating the shipment and routing of Department of Defense cargo, material and personnel within and through a 30,000 square mile area. He determined and executed the most cost-effective route and mode requirements. He was the principle coordinator and liaison for European commercial carriers, movement control agencies and other Host Nation authorities through out Western Europe. He directly managed and coordinated the movement of personnel and cargo for three REFORGER (Return of Forces to Germany) exercises, through his area of responsibly, amounting to millions of dollars and thousands of personnel effectively and efficiently arriving on schedule. Mr. Baugh was recognized for cost-effective mode selection resulting in over $12,000 a quarter in savings to the U.S. Government. He was also awarded the 1985, National Defense Transportation Association's Small Unit Award (European Division) for outstanding achievement.

Back in Fort Carson, Mr. Baugh, as Assistant Operations, Plans and Intelligence Officer, planned, coordinated and executed service and support operations for over 2,700 personnel in direct support to the 4th Infantry Division (mechanized). He directly supervised three officers, two senior non-commissioned officers, and six enlisted personnel. Mr. Baugh had an unique reservoir of institutional knowledge of the organization. He reorganized several support programs and evaluation plans that served as prototypes for subsequent programs and evaluations.

Mr. Baugh retired from the United States Army as Major in the Transportation Corps (1988).

WILFRED "BILL" BEARDSLEY

Branch of Service:
  U.S. Army
  U.S. Air Force
Years of Service:
  U.S. Army: 1/26/43 - 2/22/46 WWII
  U.S. Air Force Reserve: 2/23/46 - 9/28/50
  U.S. Air Force: 9/29/50 - 9/28/51 Korean War
  U.S. Air Force Reserve: 9/29/51 - 10/3/58
Outfit:
  "Too many to remember."
Areas Stationed:
  Stateside: Tennessee, Alabama, New Jersey, Missouri, California, Utah
  Over seas: Marshall Islands, New Guinea, Morotaii, Biak, Guam, Philippines

"I started out in the barrage balloon section of the coast artillery. After a bit I was transferred to a division in Alabama, where we trained on the 4.2 mortars. (The shoulder patch for our division was a black leopard on a circular orange background.) We went on to do maneuvers in Florida.

When I was traveling to my transfer in Ft. Leonard Wood, Missouri, I guarded a group of German prisoners that were being shipped there. They were so glad to be out of the war, they really did not need guarding.

After that, I was attached to the Air Force and transferred to a P-47 Air Base in Millville, New Jersey.

Later, I was transferred to a staging base at Kearns, Utah and then we were shipped on a troop train to Pittsburgh, California to board a troop ship in the San Francisco Bay.

We worked our way through the various islands until we wound up in the Philippines. The initial landings had already taken control of the Manila area.

As I recall, we were shipped back to San Francisco on a small ship in late January 1946. We had accumulated enough overseas points in a combat zone to be returned stateside for discharge.

I stayed in the Air Force Reserve because I liked that better than the Army.

The Korean War broke out and I was recalled to duty on September 29, 1950. All of my Korean War service through September 28, 1951, was at Robbins AFB, just outside of Macon, Georgia.

The highest rank I ever attained was Tech. Sgt. and was assigned as Sgt. Major. After my release, I stayed in the Reserves through October 3, 1958. I then figured I had done

14

my share of service.

I do not like war; I do not like the killing and maiming of good men and women. Although, for the life of me, I do not know of any other way to keep our country safe when talking does not do it. In addition, I believe that any able-bodied person should put in at least 'some' military service or our country might not be able to respond quickly enough to a threat.

I do NOT believe in any way my nearly 5-years of active service was a total waste.

On the plus side, I learned many things, and traveled to places I shall never see again.

On the minus side, I saw women with their noses and ears cut off by the enemy in the Philippines. Along with other sights one will never forget. In short, man's worst enemy is 'man' I firmly believe.

In the service I started out as an ordinary soldier, but in time I was sent to Company Clerk School, where among other things, I learned to type, and from there on I was just about 'indispensable' and didn't have to pull guard or K.P. duty. In the combat areas there is a certain amount of paper work that must be done and that was my job."

15

TONY GUY BELTRAN

Branch of Service:
> U.S. Army, Special Forces
> U.S. Marine Corps Reserves
> U.S. Army Reserves
> National Guard

Years of Service: 18 years

Outfit:
> U.S. Army, Detachment A321, 5th Special Forces
> U.S. Army Reserves, 12 Special Forces in Arizona
> Alaska National Guard, 207th Arctic Recon
> U.S. Marine Corps Reserves, Echo Company, 4th
> Marine Division

Areas Stationed:
> Fort Bragg, North Carolina; Tay Ninh, Vietnam;
> Fort Wainwright, Alaska; Elmendorf Air Force Base,
> Alaska

Deployments:
> Panama, Honduras, Hawaii

Aircraft:
> Aircraft parachuted from during military service:
> Fixed-Wing: DeHavilland Twin Otter, DeHavilland
> Caribou, C-123 Provider, C-119 Boxcar, C-130
> Hercules, C-141 Star Lifter (jet)
> Helicopters: UH-1 Huey, Ch-47 Chinook, Ch-46
> Sea Knight, UH-60 Black Hawk, H-3 Jolly Green
> Giant, H-53 Sea Stallion, S-64 Sky Crane

Specialty:
> Light Weapons Leader, Recon-Team Leader,
> Parachute Rigger, Scout, Swimmer

Mr. Beltran enlisted in the U.S. Army in 1966. After his Stateside training, he was assigned to Detachment A321, 5th Special Forces in Tay Ninh Province, Vietnam. During his tour with the detachment, he participated in numerous combat operations, mainly with Cambodian soldiers of the Civilian Irregular Defense Group. He was awarded the Bronze Star and the Combat Infantry Badge for his Vietnam Service. He also received Marine/Navy Parachute Wings, the Parachute Rigger Badge, and Parachute Wings from Vietnam, China, and Honduras. Mr. Beltran was discharged in 1969, and returned to his other career as a wild land firefighter-smokejumper. He fought fires for 28-years, 25 of those as a smokejumper, parachuting to wildfires in the Western U.S. and Alaska.

In 1980, Mr. Beltran continued his military service in the Reserves and the National Guard, joining the 12 Special Forces in Arizona. He then moved to Alaska and served with the 207th Arctic Recon. In 1985, he was asked to help form a Marine Recon Unit in Anchorage, Alaska. At age 40, Mr. Beltran left the Alaska National Guard and joined Echo Company, 4th Marine Division. He served 5-years as a Recon Team Leader and Parachute Rigger.

Mr. Beltran finished his military service as a Staff Sergeant for the Alaska National Guard, with time totaling 18-years of active and ready reserve time. He also retired from the Bureau of Land Management, Alaska Fire Service in 1994.

"Vietnam is hard to sum-up in just a few paragraphs, but I will try. I served with eight other Americans. We would rotate going on search and destroy missions with the soldiers of the Civilian Irregular Defense Group which made-up the others in the group. A mission consisted of being assigned an area by our Intelligence and we would seek out and destroy the enemy if we found him. Our foes were the Viet Cong Guerillas of the National Liberation Front.

We would leave camp at various times of the day or night. If we went by helicopter, we would air assault by day. If we went by boat or on foot, we would leave at night. When we got to our assigned area, we would try to engage the enemy in a firefight or we would set-up ambushes and lay in wait.

Depending on the nature of the threat, we would leave the camp with anywhere from 45-100 men. We always had radios to call in artillery or air strikes. We would stay out on the average of 4-6 days. Our stays were short because of the difficulties of re-supplying us in the jungle. Some of the larger, All-American units stayed out up to 30-days as they had their own air assets to support them.

Sometimes we would walk through the jungle and never see the enemy and other times we would be in a very hot

18

firefight within hours of leaving camp. It was common to run into mines and booby traps, which would tie us up for a few hours as we evacuated our wounded.

We lived in the village of Ben Soi with the Vietnamese and Cambodians. When we were not on combat operations, we would help the villagers with their farming and treat them for disease and injuries. We helped them improve the sanitation of the village so that disease wouldn't spread, and purchased pumps for them so they could have an adequate water supply.

We did not eat the same as regular American troops who had C-rations. On combat-ops, we ate mostly rice and dried shrimp or other dried fish and dehydrated vegetables, which we carried in a pouch on our belts. Add a little water and a few hours of walking and dinner was ready. Canned fruit was a special treat. I still like canned grapefruit and mandarin oranges.

My hobbies are military history, firearms and physical fitness. I am a member of the Lakeview VFW. I made a parachute jump on June 6, 2004, at the Lake County Airport, to honor the D-Day Veterans. I am also a Reserve Police Officer with the town of Lakeview. I am now training a drug detection dog (German Shepard) by the name of Dutch."

NICHOLAS BERRIMAN

Branch of Service:
   U.S. Marine Corps
   Oregon Air National Guard
Years of Service:
   U.S. Marine Corps - 1995 to 1999
   Air Guard - October 2000 to Current (5 Years)
   Operation Iraqi Freedom (2 Active Duty)
Outfit:
   U.S. Marines - Alpha Btry 1/11
   Air Guard - 173rd SFS
Areas Stationed:
   Camp Pendleton; Camp LeJuene; Klamath Falls,
   Oregon; AlAl Salem, Kuwait
Ships:
   U.S.S. Juenua (6 months)
Specialty:
   U.S. Marine Corps - Hazardous Materials
   U.S. Air Guard - Military Police

"After September 11th, I was activated in my current unit,
the 173rd Security Forces. In December of 2002, I was
deployed to Kuwait in support of Operation Enduring
Freedom, Operation Southern Watch, and Operation Iraqi
Freedom. I was able to take part in the build up process for
the Invasion of Iraq. During my 6-months in Kuwait, my
base sustained over 20 Iraqi missile attacks with no
casualties. I was fortunate to have done my part, and am
proud to serve."

JACK M. BOWERS

Branch of Service:
  U.S. Army
Years of Service:
  4 years   WWII
Outfit:
  99th Infantry Division
Areas Stationed:
  France, Belgium, Germany
Specialty:
  Field Artillery, Ground Forces

Mr. Bowers was involved in the Battle of Huertgen Forrest commonly known as the "Battle of the Bulge." He was the Aide-De-Camp to General Fredric H. Black, who was the Commander of the 99th Division Field Artillery.

"At the beginning of the battle, the Division that was next to us was completely demolished by a German Motorized Unit. The 99th Division managed to withdraw along the north side of the 'Bulge'. At the end of the 'Bulge' the American 1st Division and other Allied Forces were assembling and held the Germans from advancing farther."

Mr. Bowers was also involved in the Battle of the Rhine, The Battle of the Ruhr Valley, and the Battle of Central Europe.

GEORGE WESLEY BOYLE

Branch of Service:
> U.S. Army

Years of Service:
> 1944 - 1946   WWII

Outfit:
> 771 Tank Battalion
> U.S. Constabulary Battalion

Areas Stationed:
> Fort Knox, Kentucky and West Berlin, Germany

Specialty:
> Supply Sergeant

"Just before my 18th birthday, in April of 1944, I tried to enlist in the Navy. The previous October I had broken my leg when my horse fell on me. The Navy turned me down because I had recently broke my leg and could not do some of the exercises they put me through. Three or four months later, I was drafted into the Army. I went through basic training at Fort Knox, Kentucky. Although this was, and still is, an armored training center, I ended up there as a truck driver. After Fort Knox, I went to Europe on the Queen Mary. I was one of the 17,000 troops on the Queen. Landing in Scotland, we went by train through England to South Hampton and then across the English Channel on a ship to France. Shortly before the war ended, I joined up with the 771st Tank Battalion in southwest Germany. I count myself very lucky. During this time, I was a tank crewman, and after several moves around the American Zone, became a mail clerk. I was then sent with only a jeep driver and our officer through the English and Russian zones of Germany to Berlin. There, I was made a Supply Sergeant. During this period, our company of 771st Tank Battalion became part of the newly established 16th Constabulary Squadron. We were established as a Rapid Rendezvous Unit during the post war period."

KENNETH L. BRIGHT

Branch of Service:
   U.S. Army (SSGT)
   U.S. Army Reserve
   U.S. Air Force (TSGT)
Years of Service:
   U.S. Army:
   U.S. Air Force: 16 years
   Vietnam
Outfit:
   43rd Infantry Division
Areas Stationed:
   U.S. Army: Camp Chaffee, Arkansas; Munich,
      Germany
   U.S. Air Force: Hamilton Field, California; Kaflavik
      Island; Bitburg, Germany; Davis-Monthen, Arizona;
      McClellon, Sacramento, California
Aircraft:
   Air Force: F-89 D&H, F-104, F86D, F102, F4D&E,
   F100, U2 spy plane
Specialty:
   U.S. Army: Communications Chief
   U.S. Air Force: Aircraft Mechanic

"I took basic training at Camp Chaffee, Arkansas from January to May of 1951. I was 16-years old when I signed up, and turned 17, in the middle of Basic on March 21. I was with the 11th Air Borne for one year before going to Germany. I served as Occupational after WWII until coming home in May of 1955. I stayed in the Army Active Reserves

24

for two years then changed to the Air Force."

Mr. Bright spent 3-years on temporary duty in Ben Hou, Vietnam, 1-year in Thailand at Ubon, 3-years in Bitburg, Germany, and 2-years at Hamilton Field, California. He also spent time at Panama Canal, Clark AFB in the Philippines, Guam, Mactan, and Wake Island.

After leaving the service, Mr. Bright became a school bus driver in Oregon. He retired after 17-years to pursue travel and fishing.

Mr. Bright also served as a Reverend at the United Pentecostal Church. He retired in March 2005, after preaching the gospel for nearly 30-years.

DAVE BROWN

Branch of Service:
  U.S. Navy
Years of Service:
  4 years: Cold War and Cuban Blockade
Outfit:
  VP-16
Areas Stationed:
  Florida, Italy, New Foundland, Iceland
Aircraft:
  P2V Neptune Aircraft
Specialty:
  Pilot

"I hunted for Russian ships and submarines in the Atlantic Ocean with my P2V aircraft. I also kept track of the Russian fishing fleet, which had Russian electronics ships among them."

CHARLES ROBERT BUTLER

Branch of Service:
  U.S. Navy
Years of Service:
  1943 - 1946   WWII
Outfit:
  Lion 6 NOB 926
Areas Stationed:
  Farragut, Idaho and San Diego, California
Ships:
  M.S. Pennant (to Guam)
Specialty:
  Fireman 1st Class

"The ship we went over on was a Dutch Merchant ship. We were on the ocean 73-days. We left the states the day U.S. troops landed on Normandy, June 6, 1944. We stopped in Hawaii and the Marshall Islands. They had not taken Guam from the Japanese yet and at night, we could watch the battlewagons shelling the island. Our job was taking a landing barge to the ships to get bombs to bomb Japan.

For my next assignment, I spent 18-months working in the engine room of a yard tug.

In March 1946, I was sent back to the States, and in May of that year, I was discharged. I came back to LaGrande, Oregon, where I have been ever since."

DANIEL C. CASTILLO

Branch of Service:
U.S. Army
Years of Service:
3 years
Outfit:
1st Army, 106 Division, 60 Battalion, 424th Regiment
CB
Areas Stationed:
Fort Bliss, Texas
Ships:
Queen Mary

This is My Story
by Daniel C. Castillo
(A disabled American Veteran and Former POW)

I was in the "Battle of the Bulge". In it's entirety, the Battle of the Bulge was one of the worst battles in terms of losses to the American forces in WWII. It was the coldest and snowiest battle.

On a Wintry mid-December day in 1944, three powerful German armies plunged into the semi-mountainous, heavily forested Ardennes region of eastern Belgium and northern Luxemburg. In this battle I was wounded on my right thigh. During the battle only three of us survived from my company. We were captured by the Germans and they put us on a fire line to kill us, but they changed their mind, so we survived. After being captured we walked twenty miles to where other American soldiers were held. There they put

29

200 American G.I.s on train boxcars. They didn't give us
any food or water for two days. In prison camp, Stalag IVB,
every two weeks, one or two G.I.s were dieing of starvation
or disease. There were no medical doctors to take care of us.
We ate two cups of potato soup a day, with some dirt on the
potatoes. When we were rescued by General Patton's 3rd
Armor, an Army medical doctor tested the potato soup. He
said to the German General that not even dogs would eat the
soup, and if these soldiers stayed one more month they
would be dead of starvation. One day while still in captivity,
they sent me and another soldier to get some potatoes from
the ward house to take in a two wheeled wagon to the
kitchen. A German guard saw us eating some of the potatoes
and came running and hit us on the back of our heads with
the butt of his rifle. I have been going to V.A. Hospitals for a
long time to get treatments. I have had seven V.A. doctors
taking care of me. I am 100% disabled. In 1946, the Army
Department of Veterans Affairs sent me to a hospital in Van
Nuys, California. I was there for three months taking care of
my frozen feet, hands and ears, and also my stomach. My
feet were purple. The doctors told me they were going to cut
my two feet off. The nurses gave me some treatments and
the purple went away. The doctors sent me home and didn't
cut my feet off. I was lucky. I have been going to the V.A.
hospital for a long time. The Army Department of Veterans
Affairs Hospital of rating decisions found that I had feet
frostbite, frozen hands and ears, Arthritis, Post Traumatic
Stress Disorder, Condition of the Digestive System,
Lumbosacral Spine, Barretl's Esophagus, Gastrointestinal
Condition, Gastritis Duodenal Ulcer, Irritable Bowel
Syndrome, Hernia, Gastoesophayed Reflux. When I was
captured I weighed 145 lbs., and when I was liberated I
weighed only 90 lbs., just skin and bones. In the prison

camp were bed bugs because there was no water to take showers. Even the drinking water froze up sometimes. In the camp no one had heaters to warm the place and they had us sleeping on the floor like a dog. We did not have beds or blankets. One night a soldier went to the kitchen to get some potatoes and he hit a German guard. That night the German guards came running to get the soldiers from all the barracks because of the one soldier who hit the German guard. They took us outside. It was snowing and one foot of snow was on the ground. There we stayed about one hour. They had one submachine gun on us 200 soldiers, I guess they were going to kill all of us. They changed their mind and sent all of us inside the barracks. No wonder I got my feet frozen, hands, ears, and back too from standing for one hour on snow. One day the American Red Cross sent some food boxes for American soldiers. There was one box for each soldier, but the Germans got the boxes. They only gave us one box for each twenty men. It was a small box. We had to divide it into small pieces for each man. Here in the United States, the government took better care of all the German P.O.W.s. They had nice clean barracks, three meals a day, beds and all utilities. There are some American people who don't realize what an American soldier went through on a battlefield. You are there to kill or be killed. Also to fight for freedom from Hitler's Nazis. When the War Department of Veterans Affairs sent me for a rating to the Veterans Hospital, one psychiatric head doctor said to me that I had too much Traumatic Stress Disorder. "Forget the past of the disorder," he said, "Forget the past of the war and also the days you spent in the P.O.W. camp." I told the doctors that it was too hard to forget. After I saw American soldiers die, German tanks run over wounded soldiers, and soldiers blown to pieces.

My true story in combat.
Daniel C. Castillo
1st Army, 106 Division, 424 Regiment CB

MICHAEL WAYNE CATES

Branch of Service:
    U.S. Army (Sergeant E5)
Years of Service:
    1968 - 1970 Vietnam
Outfit:
    Company D, 1st Battalion, 12th Infantry,
    4th Infantry Division
Areas Stationed:
    PlayKoo, Ankai
Specialty:
    LB10, Light Infantry

"I went to basic training at Fort Knox, Kentucky AIT, and
Fort Polk, Louisiana, then transferred to NCO, Fort Benning,
Georgia. I did not want to be a shake and bake officer, to be
in charge of a squad on arrival to Vietnam. Therefore, I quit
the NCO program and went directly to Vietnam. On arrival
there the Captain said, "I have found the man to carry the
M-60 machine gun." For the next nine months, I was sent to
areas without any friendlies. Our job was to go in and make
sure no one was left there. We would be helicoptered there,
usually to a mountaintop. We then made our way back by
following rivers out of the area, securing as we went. I
became a Sergeant E5 there and took squads on Recon, most
of the time 4-man Recon Units. I made over 25 helicopter
drops into un-friendly areas. I had Ammo Bearers in front
and behind me. They carried 400 rounds each and I carried
300 rounds for the M-60. We would be out there from a
week to three months. We were cold and wet from the rain

33

in the jungles and were constantly on guard; because we knew, whoever was out there was there to kill us. I will not give specific details here. I wanted to live; I wanted to return to the U.S.A. I believe growing up in the country and learning to hunt and other skills helped me to survive. At this time, I am 100% disabled due to exposure to Agent Orange. I am proud to have been in the military and proud to have served my country."

PATRICK H. CHILDSON

Branch of Service:
> U.S. Marine Corps (Sgt. E-5)

Years of Service:
> November 1963 to November 1974
> Vietnam Combat 1965

Outfit:
> D-Company, 1st Battalion, 3rd Marine Division

Areas Stationed:
> Camp Pendleton, California; Santa Ana, California;
> Okinawa, Japan; Hawthorne, Nevada; Key West,
> Florida

Specialties:
> Military Police, Shore Patrol, Traffic Investigator,
> Military Police Instructor, Criminal Investigator

At the age of 18, Mr. Childson, was one of the first Marines to enter Vietnam. During his duty, he was part of a Combat Action Group. His Company was sent to DaNang in January of 1965, to guard the airstrip, run recon patrols, pickup pilots and go on town patrols looking for Viet Cong. Later, as part of the 9th Marine Expeditionary Unit, they performed combat sweep and destroy operations. In his squad, he worked as a grunt, sniper and automatic rifleman. He returned home in December of 1965, one month after his 19th birthday.

"The government still denies any combat troops in Vietnam before March 1965. My Company was sent to Vietnam prior, and then later became part of the 9th Marine Expeditionary Unit."

WILLIAM CHISHOLM

Branch of Service:
  U.S. Army
Years of Service:
  3
Outfit:
  7th Division, 31st Regiment, G-Company
Areas Stationed:
  Japan, Korea, USA
Specialty:
  Infantry, Squad Leader,
  Fired M1, Browning Automatic Riffle
  57 Recoilless, 30-caliber machine gun

Mr. Chisholm took his basic training at Fort Ord, California, went to Japan and then to Korea for one year. He was at the Chosin Reservoir in 1950, and participated in the battles at Hwachon Reservoir, Hell Fire Valley and a few other places in Korea. Mr. Chisholm finished his tour as Bayonet Instructor at Camp Roberts, California.

"Korea carries many memories for me, Inchon, rain and mud, freezing cold, a ruined countryside and the debris of war, hungry Korean children, and the Chosin Reservoir. There is only so much that a person can retain and keep his sanity. It is necessary to block out as much as possible the bad things and the bad times. Some are so bad that they will not block out. I can never forget the freezing cold, and can sometimes still hear the bugles and the whistles of the attacking Chinese. I can still recall wanting to be home where it was warm. I remember my company relieving the Marines on the ridges east of Koto-ri, and praying that both they and we would get out of there alive.

But of all the memories of Korea, the most vivid is our company attack up the finger ridge of Hill 300 near Hwachon Reservoir in central North Korea, just above the 38th parallel. The date, June 6, 1951, is burnt into my mind in letters of fire. Our attack was supported by tanks on both sides of the valley approach to the hill. As the tanks advanced, they fired upon the bunkers commanding our approaches to the hillcrest. Their fire was pretty effective. Most of the bunkers were destroyed.

Our Battalion Commander, Major Sam Holland, had called for an air strike by our jets. When we saw them, we placed our air warning panels ahead of our forward positions to indicate a no strike line behind those panels. What happened next was a mess. We were being napalmed and strafed by our own Air Force. I lost a lot of buddies that day. Sister companies in our battalion and the tank crews had a ringside seat as they watched us being fried to a crisp by our own people.

I jumped into a shattered bunker on top of some dead North Koreans just ahead of a napalm bomb that hit less than 100 feet ahead of the bunker. The blazing gunk covered the bunker. Some of it came inside and burned me on my back and legs. The intense heat blistered my face, arms-- every place except my belly since I was laying face down, my body cushioned by the dead enemy soldiers. Even there, some of the gunk seeped in to give me burns around my chest. I was unable to see for two weeks; my face was so swollen. I thought I would be blind forever. The pain was dreadful. In a Pusan hospital, I lay on my stomach for two weeks, my head cradled to keep my weight off my cooked swollen face. It was agony to even think of moving. The medics were very gentle with me, as were the gray ladies who came by daily, offering to write letters for me or read to me. They were American ladies, from where I do not know. Whether officer's wives or Red Cross workers, I remember them as angels.

I would not wish that experience on my worst enemy. I still grieve for my fallen comrades, and yet thank God that I am home and alive. I just wish that they could have lived through Chosin Reservoir and the Hwachon fighting to enjoy life and to have seen their children and grandchildren run, play and grow.

Those who have experienced napalm know that it can melt the flesh of your hands so that it resembles the yellow of a duck's foot. It just burns right through you, and there is not a damn thing you can do about it except scream and cry. My only consolation is that after that episode, jets were

39

never again used in close support of an infantry attack. The slower P-51 was substituted so that pilots had more time to identify their targets. For my burned and dead comrades that was no consolation at all.

Some two months later, in August, I returned to G2/31/7 and found a warm welcome in my old platoon. There were many new faces though. By October, I had accumulated enough points to rotate home."

DAVID COCKRELL

Branch of Service:
    U.S. Navy
Years of Service:
    3 1/2 years   WWII
Outfit:
    Landing Unit 34 (Amphibious Unit, Land and Sea)
Areas Stationed:
    South Pacific Isles
Ships:
    50ft LCM
Specialty:
    Coxswain (equal to Sergeant)

Mr. Cockrell's duties during the war consisted of transporting troops, guns, small tanks, jeeps, and supplies from ships to shore. At times, he was stationed on small islands for short periods of time.

WILMER L. COOK

Branch of Service:
    U.S. Army
Years of Service:
    1942 - 1945   WWII
    (3 years, 4 months, 18 days)
Outfit:
    531st Engineer Shore Regiment, 1st Amphibian
        Brigade
    3053rd Engineer Combat Battalion
Areas Stationed:
    North Africa; Sicily, Italy; Utah Beach, France;
    Holland (Battle of the Bulge)
Ships:
    U.S.S. Thomas A. Barry (to Ireland)
    H.M.S. Duchess of Bedford (to Africa)
Specialty:
    Machine Gunner, Mechanic

"I was 29 years-old when I was drafted into the U.S. Army, April of 1942. I left Enterprise, Oregon with 32 other boys from Wallowa County and headed for the Induction Center in Portland, Oregon. We were all sent to Monterey, California and only six of us were sent to Camp Robinson, Arkansas to begin our six-week Basic Training. When that was completed, we went to Cape Cod, Massachusetts. It was there that we formed the 531st Engineer Shore Regiment.

On July 19, we boarded the U.S.S. Thomas A. Barry bound for Ireland. Soon we traveled to Scotland where we boarded an English ship, The Duchess of Bedford, bound for North Africa.

November 9, 1942, we invaded a beach at Ouzou near Oran. I was in a machine gun squad in a defense platoon. My duty was to dis-assemble oil and re-assemble our 30-calibur machine gun. This was quite a challenge most of the time due to the sand that was whipped up by the wind and coated everything. Soon I was sent to the motor mechanic section for extra duty. This was my job of choice.

In June of 1943, our regiment took part in invading Sicily. We were in an Army DUWK when I, the crew, a 105mm Canon, and several shells were unloaded six miles from shore and 'beached' at Licata. There I cleaned and oiled the gun, and did my share of guard duty.

A year went by, and I was assigned the work of oil changing and tire repair on the trucks.

June 1943, we were loaded onto a ship for another Sicily invasion. Our 105 was towed up to the front line and fired many times in the night and the next morning sent back for more ammunition. It was not long before Sicily was flying the U.S. flag.

The men in my Army unit moved on to invade Italy at

43

Salerno Beach. A few others and I were left behind due to a bout with Malaria. When I recovered, I was put to work doing brake repair on the Army DUWKs that were affected by the salt water.

In December of 1943, we were transferred back to England to re-supply and prepare for the Normandy Invasion. My duty in England was small engine repair on the water purifying units and guard duty. I was made a Private First Class and eventually a T-5.

Thanksgiving Day, 1944, we were moved to Maastricht, Holland. Then on New Years Day, During the Battle of the Bulge, I stood guard duty for a short time.

I was discharged on August 29, 1945. I came home, met and married Mary Gillham, (the woman I had written to for the past two-years), and had five children. I worked as a rural mail carrier for 27 1/2-years in Enterprise, Oregon, and retired in 1973.

I might add that the six boys I went into the Army with all came home. When I went into the Army, I was still a laughing kid, and did not realize the seriousness of war. However, I would do it all again. I have a strong resentment against 'war protestors' and wonder where America would be today if it were not for us 9-million veterans.

On December 11, 2001, my wife passed away. She was my best friend and companion, by my side for 56-years. I miss her so much. I am 93-years old and have been making two-sided checker/Chinese checker boards out of Juniper wood to pass my lonely days. There is over one-hundred hours put into each board. I have given them to friends and family, and have donated many to local auctions for community fund raisers, 4-H, FFA, senior centers, and health care foundations."

44

America's True Heroes

Wilmer Cook, September 4, 2005

GARY COTTER

Branch of Service:
   U.S. Merchant Marine
   U.S. Army
Years of Service:
   1944 - 1953 WWII and Korean Police Action
Ships:
   S.S. Tecumseh, S.S. Don Marquis, S.S. Fort Wood,
   S.S. Ole E. Rovaag, S.S. Britain Victory, S.S. Lurline,
   S.S. Karen Olson (and many more)
Specialty:
   Oiler, Engineer, Electrician

46

"In 1944, I joined the Merchant Marine, which was under the jurisdiction of the U.S. Coast Guard. All training and upgrading examinations were administered by the U.S. Coast Guard. We sailed all waters and made every invasion that the armed forces made. I have always been very proud for the little bit that I contributed to those trying times.

I was raised in San Francisco and was still 16-years old when my mother signed the papers that allowed me to join the Merchant Marine in June of 1944. I spent one month at Catalina Island off the coast of California, learning how to row a boat and how to jump into oil-burning waters should my ship be sunk and I would have to swim away from it, as happened to many seamen during the war.

On August 17, 1944, I sailed under the Golden Gate Bridge on a ship named the S.S. Tecumseh. This was a Liberty-type vessel; hundreds of them were built during the war. My job was as an Oiler in the engine room, although, I had no training to do this job. We all ended up having on-the-job training.

On our ship, the average age was 16 or 17-years old. A few fellows were as young as 13, 14 and 15-years old. These boys were big for there age and got away with stretching the truth, as they were supposed to be at least 16, to join the Merchant Marine.

My buddy was the Fireman/Water Tender on watch with me. In addition, we had an Engineer on duty with us. He was the second Assistant Engineer, and had some sea time already.

This was the 4 PM-8 PM and the 4 AM-8 AM shift: 4 hours on duty and 8 hours off duty around the clock. There where three Oilers, three Firemen, and four Engineers, counting the Chief Engineer who did not stand a watch. Also in the Black Gang (engine room crew), was one Deck

Engineer and two Wipers (Janitors/Apprentice).

We left San Francisco and arrived in Oro Bay, New Guinea 17-days later. The only excitement was a Jap sub that chased us for about 4-days but could not get a shot at us. They had a speed of about 12-knots on the surface and so did we, thank God for that.

We ended up in Hollandia, New Guinea, and then left there for Leyte, in the Philippines. On the way to the invasion on Leyte, we had two escorts protecting us, as we had a full load of ammunition. On the way, three Jap planes attacked us and we shot all of them down. We had an armed-guard Navy gun crew with Merchant crewmembers loading for them. Merchant seamen fired some of the 20mm guns because we did not have enough Navy gunners for all guns.

We were lucky because if the Japs landed just one bomb, (on a ship full of ammunition), I would not be telling this today. I was in the engine room during the attack, which happened around daybreak. I had always heard that most attacks happen during early morning or at dusk; I guess that was good information.

When we arrived in Leyte, we immediately started to unload ammunition, as the troops needed these supplies. The fighting was just a couple miles from the harbor. I do not recall how many days we were there before being completely unloaded. Every day some Jap planes would have a go at the ships in the harbor.

My next stop was Hollandia and I was admitted into an Army Hospital. After about six weeks, I was sent to another ship located at Manus in the Admiralty Islands. I stayed on this ship for about three months before signing on to an Oil Tanker as a work-away in order to sail back to the states.

I ended up sailing on Merchant Ships until 1960. I was

drafted into the Army in 1951, for two years during the Korean Police Action. I was drafted because I was not considered a Veteran of WWII. But thank the Lord; I did not have to go to Korea. I believe that it was in 1983, the Government passed a law saying that Merchant Marines were now considered veterans of WWII. It only took them about 40-years for them to do this. I now have a U.S. Coast Guard Honorable Discharge, dated August 15, 1945.

During my seagoing years, I sailed to many places around the world, never regretting any of it."

49

JEFFERY S. CRANDALL

Branch of Service:
U.S. Marine Corps Reserves
U.S. Air Force
Wisconsin Army National Guard
U.S. Army Reserve
U.S. Army (SFC)
Years of Service:
1975 - 1997   Desert Storm
Outfit:
Tactical Air Command (U.S. Air Force)
INSCOM (U.S. Army)
Intelligence and Security Command (INSCOM)
Areas Stationed:
Arizona, Germany, Korea
Specialty:
Military Intelligence

"I enlisted in the United States Marine Corps while I was still in high school, at age 17. The USMC assigned me to the reserves waiting for me to complete high school and receive my diploma. This was in 1975, and Vietnam had wound down. The specialty I had selected for my service time was overfilled by the time I graduated and the USMC offered me either a new career field or a discharge with an opportunity to re-enlist later. I took the discharge.

Two years later, I decided to enlist in the United States Air Force. I was initially trained as a computer programmer in the early days of computer technology. My assignments were Holloman AFB, New Mexico; Langley AFB, Virginia;

Fort Huachuca, Arizona; and Davis-Monthan AFB, Arizona. Most of my years in the Air Force were spent working on special assignments and with the latest of technical equipment. I left the Air Force after almost 10-years to pursue a calling into the ministry.

My next military affiliation was with the Wisconsin Army National Guard where I was selected to attend the Wisconsin Military Academy for Officer Training School. This was an interesting school, but I was unable to complete it because my civilian job took me to Florida. I was transferred into the United States Army Reserves to complete my enlistment.

After moving to Florida, I realized how much I missed the military life and camaraderie. I decided I should enlist in the United States Army. I went on active duty and they allowed me to complete Army Basic Training, even though I had more active duty military time than any of the instructors. After basic training, I moved to Goodfellow AFB, Texas for my Advanced Individual Training in Military Intelligence. I would go on to spend eight more years in the Army working in the arena of Military Intelligence until I retired in 1997.

My first Army assignment was in Berlin, Germany, which surprised everyone since that was a coveted assignment and required a special selection. While there, I was witness to the collapse of the Berlin Wall and the withdrawal of Communist soldiers from Germany. What an experience. I met and visited with Reverend Billy Graham at the site of the Berlin Wall. My children were often mistaken for local children and had hundreds of pictures taken, by tourists, with them at the old wall using a hammer to chip it away.

When Saddam Hussein invaded Kuwait, I became very involved in the upcoming war. I was one of five soldiers in my specialty sent to Saudi Arabia from Berlin. We were hand picked by our Commander and our selection was approved by the Pentagon based on our unique skills. The trip from Berlin to Saudi Arabia was an experience in itself. We had to be flown back to Fort Knox, Kentucky, and were imbedded into a group of Army Reserve soldiers who had been recalled to active duty. Our orders were changed so we were no longer from Berlin and had new Military Occupation Specialties. Once we arrived in Saudi Arabia, via TWA, we were again separated from the reserve soldiers and sent to the Army Headquarters in Riyadh, Saudi Arabia. Although my time during Desert Storm was spent behind the lines it was still was very interesting. We were bombed frequently with SCUD missiles from Iraq and watched our Patriot Missile crews explode them overhead. We were not prepared for the results of the fallout from these missiles, as many of us are now combating illnesses which doctors cannot identify their cause. I worked with the communications equipment at the headquarters and transmitted the message to the forward commanders to start the ground offensive, which lasted four days. The return to Berlin from Saudi Arabia was also a trip worth remembering. I used my Air Force background to secure a flight from Saudi Arabia and we went to Spain. From there we flew to southern Germany and then took a bus around Germany and finally to Frankfurt. From Frankfurt we road another bus into Berlin and I convinced the bus driver to stop at an unscheduled location where I had arranged to have our wives and commanders meet us. There was a reception team waiting at the bus station and we were not interested in meeting them after what we had just been through.

On March 1, 1992, at midnight, Field Station Berlin was officially closed. At that time, I was the team leader of the midnight shift and I sent the message to the world that we were now closed. Field Station Berlin had been a forward collection and monitoring station for the duration of the Cold War and this was the signal the Cold War was over.

The remaining years I spent in the Army saw me being requested as the Military Intelligence support for actions in Bosnia and Somalia. I also worked with a training team traveling around the world training Military Intelligence soldiers on a new computer system designed to assist them in their duties. Finally, I was sent to Korea for a year where I was responsible for bringing into action the computer system I had been teaching. This was the first implementation of this system for daily use in a volatile environment."

JAMES B. CRAWFORD

Branch of Service:
    U.S. Army   (Chief Warrant Officer CW-2)
Years of Service:
    November 1966 - April 1970   Vietnam War
Outfit:
    213th Assault Support Helicopter Company "The
    Black Cats of Phu Loi"
Areas Stationed:
    Phu Loi, Republic of Vietnam
Aircraft:
    CH-47 Chinook Helicopter
Specialty:
    Aircraft Commander, Chief Instructor Pilot, Safety
    Officer

"The Chinook was a tandem-rotor heavy lift helicopter used to deliver troops and supplies to the front lines. Most loads were carried externally on the cargo hook (food, water, ammunition, vehicles, and Howitzers, etc). Jeeps and 3/4 ton trucks could be carried internally.

From January of 1968 to April of 1970, I logged over 2,000 combat flying hours. My helicopter was hit by enemy fire on four occasions, but I was never wounded. My roommate and his entire crew of six were killed in action in 1969.

I am proud to have served and happy to be home!"

GEOFF DARLING

Branch of Service:
    U.S. Army
Years of Service:
    1968 - 1971
    Vietnam 1969 - 1970
Outfit:
    121st Assault Helicopter Company
Areas Stationed:
    Soc Trang Army Air Field, Vietnam
Aircraft:
    UH-1D Utility Helicopter
    UH-1B Gunship
Specialty:
    Aircraft Commander, Fire Team Lead

Mr. Darling went into the Army immediately after graduating from high school, specifically to become a helicopter pilot. He was 19, when he graduated from the Army Aviation School and was commissioned as a Warrant Officer, then he was sent immediately to Vietnam. Mr. Darling flew troop carriers on combat assaults and medical evacuations supporting the South Vietnamese Army Units, U.S. Army advisers, U.S. Army Special-Forces Teams, and U.S. Navy Seal Teams. He transferred to the gunship platoon and flew UH-1B Huey Gunships. He spent 11 months and 28 days in Vietnam. He later became an instructor pilot at Fort Rucker, Alabama. Mr. Darling left the Army in 1971, and then entered college.

EDWIN A. DAVIS

Branch of Service:
>   U.S. Army Corps of Engineers   (S/Sgt)
>   U.S. Navy

Years of Service:
>   U.S. Army: 4 years
>>   Korea: 1950 - 1953 (two tours)
>   U.S. Navy: 24 1/2 years (Attack Pilot)
>>   Cuban Crisis
>>   Vietnam

Areas Stationed:
>   Pensacola, Florida; Brunswick, Maine; Puerto Rico;
>   Sicily; Spain; Corpus Christi and Kingsville, Texas;
>   Lemoore, Los Angeles and San Diego,
>   California; Philippines; Japan; and the entire
>   country of Korea.

Ships and Aircraft:
>   Vietnam era: USS Hancock CVA-19 (Attack Pilot -
>   flew A-4E and F attack jets - 126 combat missions)
>   Post Vietnam: USS Ranger CV-61 (Air Department
>   Officer - Air Boss)
>   Also flown: T-34, T-28, T2V, P2V-7, H-34, HU2,
>   F9F-8, SNB, A-4C, A-4E/F, A-7A &B
>   Over 6,000 hours and 650 carrier landings

Specialty:
>   Army: Demolitions Specialist.   Armed and de-armed
>   personnel and vehicle mines, and was proficient in
>   the use of all explosives in all situations. Was on
>   3.5 in. bazooka team and a .30 cal light machine
>   gun team.

Navy: Trained in the use of all air-launched air-to-ground conventional and nuclear weapons.

"I joined the Army in March of 1950, when I was 15-years old. It's called a fraudulent enlistment. I lied about my age, and how I did that is another story. Joining the Army was my way out of a bad home life. I completed Infantry Basic at Fort Knox, Kentucky and was home on leave when the Korean War broke out. I had orders to Fort Belvoir, Virginia for Demolition School. Upon completion of that six-week school, I was shipped overseas to Japan and then was embarked on another troop ship to Korea. I went over the side into a landing craft at Wonsan on a cold November morning. On the beach, I was directed for transport to my assigned unit, 44th Engineers, X Corps that had already advanced to Hamhung in the north. Shortly after my reporting to A Company, the C.C.F. launched a decisive attack taking Wonsan now to our south cutting us off with our backs to the sea. The resulting Battle of The Chosin Reservoir means much to our countries' military history. What happened in those 27-days is taught in every military school and senior command college. It ranks with the Battle of the Bulge and Thermopylae for ferocity, commitment and courage."

BATTLE OF THE CHOSIN RESERVOIR
November 27 - December 24, 1950

On the east side of the mountains, U.N. troops advanced north to the Chosin (Changjin) Reservoir, some 78-miles of twisting narrow dirt road from the coastal city of Hungnam. There, about 30-miles below the Yalu River, the 1st Marine Division (reinforced), two Battalions of the U.S. Army's 7th Division and a force of British Royal Marine Commandos, comprising of about 15,000 men of the X (Tenth) Corps, were surrounded by 120,000 Chinese troops.

The C.C.F. had isolated the trapped forces into four main groups and set up roadblocks all along the road. The battle was fought in minus 30-degree weather beginning November 27, 1950, until the U.N. forces had fought their way through one roadblock after another, reaching Hungnam on December 11. The Marines and Army continued to fight, as platoons were reduced to squads.

The tents used for sickbay were not nearly large enough to hold the wounded. The less critical were heaped outside in piles and covered with canvas and straw. Doctors and surgeons worked in a frenzy over the wounded. Blood plasma was frozen and could not be used. Surgeons and Navy Hospital Corpsmen were burdened by having to wear gloves and the morphine syrettes could not be used unless held in their mouths to unfreeze.

As impossible as it may seem, the Division managed to fight its way to the sea, bringing its dead, wounded and equipment. In this epic battle, the 15,000 allies suffered 12,000 casualties including more than 3,000 KIA, 6,000 WIA, and thousands of severe frostbite cases, while the enemy sustained more than 45,000 casualties.

A total of seventeen Medals of Honor, seventy Navy Crosses plus many Distinguished Service Crosses were awarded for the campaign, the most for a single battle in U.S. Military history. Survival of the ground troops was due in great part to the gallant air strikes by the U.S. Navy, Marine and Air Force fliers under the most adverse weather conditions. By December 24, the Tenth Corps was successfully evacuated to South Korea by the U.S. Navy and the U.S. Air Force along with nearly 100,000 North Korean civilian refugees.

-End of synopsis

"My feet were frostbitten, yet I continued to function and was evacuated from Hungnam around December 23rd or 24th, via a Navy LST as Chinese patrols were entering the city. We burned all supplies that would burn and blew up everything that would not so that the Chinese could make no use of them. I also helped booby-trap everything that they might touch. We buried or concealed large caches of explosives with chemical timed detonators attached to explode weeks later.

The synopsis above makes little mention of the 7th Division troops. Of the two battalions, not more than 400 made it out alive. They were poorly led and badly organized. My best friend, Jimmy Riddell was killed at the Reservoir. I named my second son, James, in his honor. Although a soldier, I cannot say enough about the Marines. They were proud, superbly led, and continued to fight, even when their ammo ran out. They fought with knives, shovels, their fists and weapons they ripped out of the hands of the enemy. That was the basis for so many MOH's.

I returned to Korea for a second tour in 1952, and was there when the cease-fire was signed. I was 19-years old when I was discharged from the Army with the rank of S/Sgt and four years of service. Based on very high GED scores, I was admitted to Michigan State University in 1954, and graduated in 1958. Missing the camaraderie of the service, I entered the Navy Flight Program in 1960, and was commissioned an Ensign receiving my gold Navy wings in 1961. I flew patrol bombers my first tour, instructed flight students my second tour, and transitioned into jets following that. I made three combat cruises on the U.S.S. Hancock, bombing many ground targets in North and South Vietnam,

and Laos. I chased a MIG-21 one time, but he got away. I
flew the last U.S. aircraft mission to receive AAA fire
occurring months after the war ended.

I loved serving my country and associating with our
countries heroes. I think of one or more every day of my life.
I love my life. I savor the sunshine and the sweet smell of
the morning air. I love looking at this beautiful world of
ours, but I never forget some of the other things I have seen.
Remember, no one hates war more than the warrior.
However, it is the warrior that has given our freedoms we
enjoy and who has repeatedly moved the ramparts to protect
those freedoms time and time again. God Bless America."

SAMUEL W. DAWSON

Branch of Service:
>U.S. Army (Sergeant First Class)

Years of Service:
>20 years, 2 months

Outfit:
>213th Field Artillery (Korea), 2nd Division, 4th Division
>5th division, (USA) General Deport, Alaska and Germany
>4th Battalion, 12th Infantry 199th Infantry Brigade; 6th Army Training Center, 8th Division

Areas Stationed:
>Fort Jackson, South Carolina; Korea; Fort Lewis, Washington; Alaska; Japan; Germany; Vietnam; Fort Carson, Colorado

Ships:
>Troop carrier: U.S.S. General Anderson and U.S.S. General Geiger

Specialty:
>Logistics, Chemical, Combat Intelligence, Drill Sergeant

Mr. Dawson entered the Army in April of 1953. His initial training was at Fort Jackson, South Carolina.

He served in both the Korean and Vietnam wars. One of his memories of Korea was the very cold weather. Although he did not see much action in Korea, he saw plenty in Vietnam, for which he received an Army Commendation Medal, Purple Heart, Combat Infantryman Badge and others.

Mr. Dawson enjoyed working in the Chemical, Biological, and Radiological field as well as in Combat Intelligence. After his return from Vietnam, Mr. Dawson trained young civilian men to be soldiers. During his many travels with the Army, he learned to speak parts of the Korean, Japanese, and German languages.

ROBERT DLOUHY

Branch of Service:
U.S. Marine Corps   (Sergeant)
U.S. Marine Corps Reserves
Years of Service:
1946 to 1947 - U.S.M.C.
1950 to 1952 - U.S.M.C.R.
Outfit:
H&S Company, 2nd Battalion, 5th Marines, 1st Marine, Division
Areas Stationed:
San Diego, California (1946 - 1947)
Korea (1951 - 1952)
Aircraft:
One of the first Battalions moved off line by helicopter
Specialty:
Radio Operator (SCR 300 - 39 1/2 pounds)

Sergeant Robert Dlouhy (left) and Sergeant Mike Dunn

"I joined the United States Marine Corps in 1946, one day after my high school graduation. I was discharged from active service in 1947, and returned home to begin the apprentice electrician program. I was still in the U.S.M.C. but in the inactive reserve for the next four-years.

In November of 1950, I received orders to report to Camp Pendleton in California for active service. At this time, my wife was pregnant with our first child. I caught the train in Seattle, and reported to Camp Pendleton with 1,800, other recalled veterans to form the sixth replacement draft. After a short refresher course in basics, we left San Diego in February 1951, aboard the U.S.S. Randall troopship. We took the southern route to Japan and arrived in Kobe after 13-days at sea. Here we dropped our sea bags and personal gear and exchanged our American money for G.I. script. Military personnel were not allowed to carry cash into war.

We left Kobe and arrived in Pusan, Korea on March 1, where we boarded a narrow gauge railroad train that was to take us to Tajeon and the front line. I was assigned to H&S Co., 2nd Battalion, 5th Marine Regiment, as Radio Operator.

The SCR-300 Radio that I carried had a head set with an earmuff, which I wore at all times, awake or sleeping, changing from one ear to the other. There was a constant hissing sound if there was not voice communication. The minute someone pushed the key to speak the hissing stopped and you could hear their voice. After many months of shhhhh in your ear, your regular hearing was not very good. The radio itself weighed 39 1/2 pounds and was mounted on a pack board. In addition to the radio, I carried a small pack with 2 pair of socks, 2 pair of shorts, 2 T-shirts, a shaving kit, a sleeping bag, a shelter half, a .45 cal. pistol, a carbine rifle with two magazines of 30-rounds of ammunition each, and usually a C-ration to eat. In the

Marine Corps, you have a buddy system for shelter. Mike Dunn, (now deceased) was my buddy who carried the other half of the shelter. Snapped together, it almost made a small tent usually placed over our foxhole for two.

Operation 'Ripper' was starting and I was assigned to carry radio for Captain Mayer. My first day with Easy Company was on the front lines standing on a ridge that we had just taken over. A young Marine was standing next to me when a North Korean sniper shot him through his helmet into his head and he died instantly. That being said, I decided that if it were going to be the enemy or me, it would definitely not be me.

Our objective was to take Hongchon and Chonchon. First, we had to clear out Hoengsong in the snow. While advancing north, we waded across streams and there was never enough time to stop and empty the water from your boots. After several hours of hiking with boots full of water, the feet would become water shriveled. During the winter and the freezing weather, the water stayed warm in the Arctic boots we had the second winter. During the first winter, the ShoePacs allowed your feet to freeze inside your boots.

We went many times without rations for several days. Sometimes we would receive an airdrop. One time it was gunnysacks full of hard-boiled eggs, but they were not peeled and the shells and eggs were all mashed together. One time it was lettuce; what were they thinking? A few times when we were desperate, we would cut the bandoleer of rice from a dead C.C.F. The bandoleer was like a long stocking worn diagonally across the chest and tied in the front. If we were in the right place, we could actually light a small fire, boil water and cook the rice.

One of the important things we learned was how to dig a

foxhole. A great deal of land in Korea is rice paddies that are fertilized with human waste. There was a constant 'stink'. Their toilets were very large pottery vases buried in the ground with the opening level with the ground. These were just outside of the houses. During night patrols, many a Marine fell into one of these 'honey pots'.

On the final phase of Operation 'Ripper,' on March 14, encountering stiff resistance, we moved from Line Buffalo to Line Cairo, gaining about 35-miles and 20-miles of front line in the last 3-weeks. We re-crossed the 38th parallel by April 4, crossed the Soyang-Gang River, and headed for Line Quantico north of the Hwachon Reservoir. At this time, I was assigned to carry radio for the S3 Officer Major Averill and I received word that I was a father of a baby girl.

We received a C-7 ration everyday if we were in an area where this was available. A C-7 box ration has one of five 'heavies': either pork and beans, or corned beef hash, or meat and noodles, or rice and vegetables, or two hamburger patties. This food tastes pretty good when you can heat it, but most of the time you cannot have a fire because you are on the frontline, so you eat it cold. There is a small can of fruit cocktail, cocoa in a packet, instant coffee packet, powered milk packet, Chiclets gum, 5 Camel cigarettes, one can opener, and about 10 squares of toilet paper.

General Douglas MacArthur was relieved of his duty by General Van Fleet. On April 23, the C.C.F. started the fifth phase offensive and hit the R.O.K. (Republic of Korea) Division on our left flank. The R.O.K. proceeded to throw down their weapons and run while the K.M.C. (Korean Marine Corps) on our right flank held their ground. The 7th Marine Division was called up to plug the left flank so that the all Marine Regiments, including the K.M.C. could make a strategic withdrawal back to Line Kansas. All regiments were back by April 24, and by the 26th, we had moved back to ChonChon and the south bank of the Soyang-Gang River.

After the first crossing of the river, the North Koreans had opened the floodgates, flooding the river and tried to destroy our pontoon bridges. In order to re-cross the Soyang-Gang, the bridges were replaced and the Naval Air torpedoed the floodgates at the Hwachon Dam so the water would flow in a steady stream instead of flood stage. During all of this battle and withdrawal, we had to repulse wave after wave of C.C.F. with their bugle calls, green and red flares, whistles, singing, humming, chanting, and god-awful yelling.

The United Nation personnel troops consisted of U.S.A., United Kingdom, Australia, Turkey, Philippine Islands, Thailand, Canada, New Zealand, Greece, France, Belgium, Luxembourg, Ethiopia (men and women) and the Netherlands. Minus the U.S. troops, the U.N. troops numbered about 22,000. The U.S. troops totaled about 222,000 and the R.O.K. about 249,000. The U.N. estimate of enemy casualties ranged from 70,000, to 100,000. The fifth phase was defeated.

The USMC troops were located on the east side of Korea, which is mostly mountainous. To get from one location to another, we hiked by foot. It was not uncommon to start hiking at 5:00 A.M., continue all day, and through the night until next morning with a ten minute break every hour. A battalion could be stretched out for miles. The best place to be was up front and that is where the Radioman, (I), was with the man in charge (the Major).

From May 4, to May 20, there were day patrols some for one day, others for two or three days. On the 20th, we had been out nine-days in no-man's-land looking for the enemy when we encountered a company or more of men in the

68

process of changing from their blue uniform clothes to civilian clothing. They were on a knoll directly below our ridgeline. Our S3 Officer gave order to open up with everything we had and that ended that group. Then we returned to the front line.

On May 25, we moved about 7,000-yards north of Hangye and then on the 26th and 27th, to Kortiw-Gol. The next four-days moved us 6,000-yards to a position northeast of Yanggyu, north of the 38th parallel and above Inje. The United Nations count from the 15th to May 31 estimated enemy casualties of 105,000, including 17,000, counted dead and 10,000, prisoners. Losses for the 1st Marine Division during May were 75, KIA (Killed in Action) and 731, WIA (Wounded in Action).

On June 1, we headed north for Line Kansas with very little resistance and pushed ahead 5,000-yards northeast to Hill 610, for 10-days. 1/5 and 2/5, slugged it out with the C.C.F. and climbed about 1,200-feet, then descended 1,200-feet five times while advancing.

On June 11, we went back from the front to regimental reserve. We received a beer ration once in awhile when in reserve; three cans at $.50 per can. It came in a khaki can, Shaffer's Beer. June 25, was the first anniversary of the Korean Conflict. Truce talks began again and I was promoted to Corporal.

On July 17, the Division returned to reserve at Inje. On August 27, we were out of reserve and followed the seventh regiment up the Soyang Valley to the Punchbowl. Then on September 1, the 5th Marines were patrolling the division zone along the Kansas Line and protecting defense installations. By September 2, N.K.P.A. was pouring in artillery and mortar fire equal to the Marine and Army sent north. (The C.C.F. is the Chinese Communist Forces, and the N.K.P.A. is North Korean Peoples Army) and combined we called either force 'gooks'.

Only human transport, no motor vehicles, was available for supplying Marines on the firing line with ammunition and C-7 rations. It took one full day for the Korean Civil Corps to complete a supply trip from battalion to the front lines. During the summer, it is very hot and winters can be very cold, with up to 12-inches of snow. This Korean Service Corps consisted of about 20,000-civilian Korean laborers hauling their 'A' frames on their backs with water, rations, ammunition, mail from home, batteries for radios (my SCR-300 used batteries that weighed 15-pounds apiece). Almost all of the terrain is steep and in the mountains. We relied heavily on these people for supplies.

September 6, the 12th Replacement Draft arrived and on September 14, with loss of 300-casualties for the 1st Marines, 300-casualties for the 7th Marines, the 5th Marines moved back onto the front line.

On September 15, the Major, two Sergeants and I moved up to the front lines with Easy Company. The Major was acting as the S3 Officer directing action on the line. Our objective was to secure Hill 812, 'The Rock'. Mortar fire, hand grenades, artillery, machine gun fire and hand-to-hand combat lasted five long days. This was the last major offensive of the Korean War; no more forward troop movement. We had established and held our position.

September 23, the day after the last major offensive, the 1st Marine Division goes into division reserve and October 6, Major Averill was transferred to Division. I had been teaching radio off and on since September to the replacements. Then on November 10, the 2nd Battalion, 5th Marines were to relieve the 1st Marines on line by helicopter, five men at a time, VMO-6. We started in the morning and finished late noon. Our position was on the east coast Sint-Awlni in North Korea. On November 14, I was made Sergeant.

December 6, the 15th Replacement Draft arrived. January 6, 1952, the artillery sent a present of 37,000, rounds to the C.C.F. on Hill 1352, Ao-Mu-An. On January 10, the division went into reserve at Camp Tripoli.

Then from January 13 to 16th, we went looking for C.C.F. guerillas and February 9, back on line on the east coast with supporting fire from naval gunfire from the Battleship New Jersey standing by in the Japanese Sea.

We had a few snipers in our outfit with '03' rifles fixed with scopes the length of the barrel. The range of this weapon was 1,000-yards. These snipers would sneak out through out line into enemy territory and lay hidden all day waiting for the enemy to expose himself. When they were in reserve it was practice and more practice sharp shooting.

February 20, replacements arrived. On February 27, an observation plane reported that on Luke's Castle, which was in front of Easy Company, yards and yards of dirt were spotted coming out of the mountain. There was a call for air support of B-29 planes to bomb this area since it was apparent that the enemy was tunneling toward our line. Then, on February 29, a B-29 that was headed for Yalu caught on fire and crashed in front of our lines. There were no survivors.

On March 10, we were relieved from the front lines by the 3rd Battalion, 5th Marines, and went into regiment reserve. During the time I was in Korea, we never lost a man to the enemy. We went beyond the front line, if necessary, to retrieve our comrades, wounded or dead, and returned them to our unit.

On March 15, I received orders to go home, leaving the

América's True Heroes

2nd Battalion for So-Cho-Ri. On March 19, I arrived at So-Cho-Ri and the next morning boarded a LST for Japan. However, before we left Korea, we were all fumigated with DDT powder from head to foot. We all looked like white powder zombies. We arrived in Kobe, Japan on the 21st to board the General W.H. Gordon U.S.N.S. We picked up our sea bags, and personal gear that we had left there in 1950. After one day of liberty, we began to sail toward San Francisco.

We were the 14th Replacement Draft to head home from Korea. We were 800-men returning after 13-months on the front lines from the original 1,800, which had arrived in 1951. After 12-days on very rough seas (the tail end of two typhoons), we arrived in San Francisco Harbor. Our big welcome home party was one elderly woman offering coffee. We then boarded a naval ferry to Treasure Island where we were to eat our first real food (anything we wanted) and get our orders to return to our homes. They gave us one night liberty in Oakland or San Francisco. I hopped a plane for home where my wife met me and introduced me to my daughter, who was now one-year old.

After 30-days, I was discharged from the USMC and returned to my job as an electrician. Some of the people that I had worked with before I went to Korea asked me where I had been. They did not seem to realize that there had been a war called the Korean Police Action and that many were wounded or had died while they were at home, blissfully unaware."

RODERICK DONNELLY

Branch of Service:
U.S. Navy
Years of Service:
February 11, 1942 to November 25, 1945
WWII
Areas Stationed:
Bremerton, WA (Naval Base)
Stillwater, OK (Navy School)
Corpus Christie, TX (Navy School)
San Diego, CA; North Island Naval Air Station
San Diego, CA; Miramar Naval Air Station
Oahu, HI; Kaneohe Bay Naval Air Station
Marianas Islands, Tinian Island, North Field
Philippines, Leyte Island
Philippines, Mindoro Island
Maryland, Patuxent River Naval Air Station
Ships or Aircraft:
"I was overseas with Navy Patrol Bombing
Squadron, UPB-117."
Specialty:
Aviation Radar Technician

"My experiences were very ordinary. I enlisted in
Portland, Oregon on February 11, 1942. Since I had a HAM
(Amateur Radio) license, I was sent to two Technician
Schools. Upon graduation, I was sent to NAS, North Island
in San Diego where several others and I were to teach
Aviation Radar Operation and maintenance to pilots and
radiomen who were headed off to the Pacific Fleet. In

February of 1944, I was transferred to VPB-117 (Patrol
Bombing Squadron 117) where I was placed in a plane crew
as a radar operator and waist gunner. When we finished our
preliminary training at Miramar, the squadron was
transferred to Kaneohe Bay NAS on the Island of Oahu.
Upon completion of further training, we were transferred to
Tinian Island in the Marianas group. From there we flew
patrols over that part of the Pacific and up around the Bonin
Islands (Iwo Jima, etc.) When the first airstrip became
operational in the Philippines, we went to the island of
Leyte. We were the first heavy bombing squadron back in
the Philippines. From there we went to the island of
Mindoro. We ran patrols extending from Southern Borneo
to as far as Okinawa. The first of April 1945, I was rotated
back to the United States. During this time, the crew that I
was in had shot down four Japanese planes and sank two
ships. Later VPB-117 was credited with the best combat
record of all the Navy squadrons serving in the Pacific. No
one in our crew received as much as a scratch although the
plane was damaged several times.

After a two-month leave, I was assigned to NAS Patuxent
River, Maryland. This was the Navy's test and experimental
base, comparable to the Army's Wright-Patterson Base in
Ohio. There I was placed in a small unit whose job was to
find the source of interference and noise in a planes radio
communication equipment and find a remedy. This
continued until the war ended and I was transferred back to
Bremerton and discharged on November 25, 1945.

I have been asked if we aircrew saw much action? The
answer is no, not always. We had many routine patrols
where nothing happened.

A typical flight would go like this: At Leyte, we were

assigned Sector Sugar, which took us to the Mekong River and Condor Island and was the longest patrol. If we were scheduled for a 3:00 A.M. flight take-off, we would have a 1:30 A.M. wake-up call. We would get our gear together and go to the mess tent for breakfast, and then to the airstrip to preflight our plane. If we were lucky to have 833, the good one, and then if preflight went fast, we might beat the 3:00 A.M. by fifteen minutes. The engines are started and we taxi to the end of the runway, swing into position and run up the engines for a magneto check. Everything looks good, so the brakes are set and the engines run up to full take off power. You make sure the waist hatches, wind deflectors and cowl flaps are closed. Flaps are set at half flap position. You hear and feel the deep almost bone shaking roar that you get from those big radial engines when you are trying to lift a big oversized load off that too short metal strip. The brakes are released and we start to roll. It sounds like we are running through a garbage dump. Just as we get to take off speed, the plane lifts off; the noise disappears and then returns as the plane settles back. Then it lifts off again and stays off. We start a gradual climb, the gear comes up with a thump, and then the plane sinks momentarily as the flaps are raised. Our speed builds and we have gained enough altitude to start a gentle left turn to let us follow the Strait west over the Visayan Sea. I have had the radar gear on warming up and as soon as the wheels and flaps are up, George Evanovich, our port gunner and 1st Ordinance man, cranks the antenna down for me. It is still dark and at this time, we aren't concerned about enemy fighters. I am on the radar watching for any enemy shipping that might be present. We take a compass heading of about 290-degrees true and grind away on our flight. The guns are test fired and our Ordinance man goes into the bomb bays and arms our bombs. The

fuses are screwed into the nose of the bombs (we are
carrying six-five hundred pounders) and safety wires are put
in place. The fuses have a built in four-five second delay so
that when you drop them at low altitude, you are clear before
they explode. A bomb that went off on contact would
probably get you as well as the target. The bombs are
carried in the two after bomb bays. The two forward bays
carry two-four hundred-gallon auxiliary fuel tanks. The
fuses aren't placed in the bomb until we are up and on our
way. The idea being, if we crashed on take off, there is less
chance of a bomb explosion. I really don't know how much
good that would do us, but it sounds good. If we don't use
our bombs on targets, we will defuse them and salvo them
into the ocean before we land. We had plenty of bombs, so
salvoing them gave us a safety factor on landing. A defused
bomb may be as inert as a chunk of concrete, but if the plane
crashed on landing and burned, they could cook off.

We would climb slowly, passing over Northern Cebu,
Negros, Southern Panay, over Northern Palawan and out
into the South China Sea. We want to hit the Indo-China
Coast at Na-Trang and then turn south on our cross leg. I
kept track of our whereabouts and let the pilot know when
and where we cross Palawan. There is nothing now until we
reach Asia. When it gets light, we can see there is enough
wind to raise some white caps, so I scramble through the
bomb bays to the drift sight (an instrument that tells you if
wind is blowing you off course) and take a reading. We have
10-degrees right drift. We assume we have had this for the
last half-hour and compensate by changing course 20-
degrees to the left for the next half-hour. Another drift sight
reveals there are no more white caps. All this proves is that
there is no surface wind. We are at four thousand feet and
we might be getting some drift, but we can't determine how

much. We return to our original heading and continue grinding along our way. No problems, the radar shows nothing. Finally, at about the expected time, I get returns on the edge of the one hundred-mile range and it is Asia. By the time we are down to fifty miles, I have identified our landfall. We will come in about twenty miles north of Na-Trang. We didn't compensate quite enough for our crosswind drift. A slight course correction takes care of that. We start to lose altitude and settle out at five hundred feet and head south on our cross leg. We stayed a half-mile or so off shore. The day is clear and visibility is excellent. There is nothing of note. There are a few small fishing boats. Soon we come up on Cap St. Jacques. This is where the Mekong River comes into the sea. There are several channels through the large delta. This is the dry season and the water that is there is in the channels, leaving plenty of farmland in between the channels that during the rainy season would be under water. At one place there are a few grass sided and thatched huts up on stilts, probably twelve to fifteen feet above the ground. At one place, a farmer is working in a garden. He is wearing a large hat and when we go over him, he doesn't even look up.

We then turned almost due south and head for Condore Island. This is a small but very steep volcanic rock island. There were phosphate mines there during pre-war times and has a good harbor. If everything goes well with us, we use it as our turn around point. There is nothing there that needs to be shot at or bombed so we turn and head for home. We open our box of ten in one rations and have lunch. Gradually, we climb back to eight thousand feet and grind away for home base. There is no land ahead of us for several hours and the radar shows me nothing. As we approach the Philippines, we gradually let down to about five hundred

77

feet. It is still daylight and we need to be alert for fighters. We see nothing and swing into the Strait between Leyte and Samar, turn toward the strip, put gear and flaps down, crank up the radar antenna, and land. It has been fourteen hours and eighteen minutes after we lifted off until touch down. We turn on the taxiway and park on an empty space. A jeep comes up and takes the pilot away to the intelligence tent for de-briefing. The plane captain notes any items to be corrected to the fellow there from the service unit. In this case he signs the 'squawk sheet' off as 'no discrepancies' and we are through for the day. We get our own personal gear from the plane, get in a weapons carrier and are taken to the tent area. This is a more typical flight than one that has all kinds of action. We haven't seen anything of military value, but we have looked at a sizeable area and know there is nothing there and this in itself is valuable knowledge.

A word about the equipment we used. The planes were the B24-J models. Various contractors made them and various changes were made as time went on. Four Pratt and Whitney R 1830-65 engines powered them. 'R' for radial, 1830 was the number of cubic inches each engine displaced and 65 represented the number of changes made to the engines since they were first introduced. These were an eighteen cylinder, two-row radial and were fitted with a three bladed Hamilton-Standard metal propeller. The engines were air cooled and very reliable. They had been in use long enough to have the 'bugs' worked out. They were used on many other types of aircraft. They were rated at one thousand one hundred-horse power with a 'War Emergency Rating' of one thousand six hundred-horse power. The latter engines settings were used only in case of dire emergency and for as short period of time as possible. Our engines were modified to the extent of removing the high altitude carburetors that the Army Air Corps used and were replaced with ones that worked best at relatively low altitudes (approximately zero to fourteen thousand feet). A plane carried three powered turrets with two .50 Caliber Browning designed guns each. The bow turret was made by ERCO (Engineering Research Corporation) and was electrically driven. The top turret was made by Martin and was electrically powered. The tail turret was made by Consolidated Aircraft and was driven by a hydraulic motor of fifteen horsepower. Each waist hatch carried a single free mounted gun. The port and starboard waist gunners could move these for various angles of shooting. The radar antenna on our planes replaced the position used by the belly turret on the Army Air Corps planes, and this was raised and lowered, as the belly turret would have been, by a manual crank. Most of the radio gear was Army Air Corps equipment. Our radar was the most advanced set available. The planes' wingspan was one hundred ten feet, length sixty-seven feet, and wing area one thousand forty-eight square feet. The empty weight was thirty-six thousand nine pounds. This last is very conservative, as we regularly flew hundred fifty pounds and gross weight was sixty thousand pounds. This last is very conservative, as we regularly flew them at sixty-eight thousand pounds and one Army Air Corps pilot I talked with said they regularly flew them off a matting strip at Biak at seventy-two thousand pounds. The wing loading was sixty-five pounds per square foot at sixty-eight thousand pounds. Maximum speed was listed at two hundred seventy-nine MPH, and maximum range at two thousand nine hundred sixty miles. Both of the latter, as we flew them, were high ratings.

Our parachutes were chest packs. We wore our harness and the chutes were held in place by bungee cords near our stations. It was only a moment's work to grab one and snap it in place. We also were given flak suits. They each weighed about seventy-five pounds. I wore mine just once, when we saw something up by Iwo Jima. We made a sharp turn and I just slumped down to the deck and stayed there until we straightened up. After that, I put it on my seat and sat on it. The first time it was necessary to jettison weight, they were the first thing thrown overboard. If something happened, there wasn't time to put them on, they limited your mobility, and I don't know of any instance where wearing one would have made any difference. We were each issued a Smith and Wesson Victory Model .38 Special and a shoulder holster. We also had a sheath knife, commonly called a 'shark knife'. These were of good quality and I still have mine. We were given a survival kit that had a 'pointee talkee' book in several Asian languages. A waterproof piece of cloth with an American flag on it and again in several languages, saying that we were an American and that the U.S. Government would pay a greater amount of money for our safe return, more than anything the Japs would offer. In addition, a packet containing fifty thousand dollars in Chinese money in case we needed spending money. I still have one of the bills and guess it is still valid. We didn't wear the .38's in the plane. We had them, and they were intended to take with us if we were forced down or had to bail out. We had a 'Mae West' on board and if needed, the chute harness went over it. These also were at the appropriate places. You might have to check and adjust the chute harness. All of these things were items checked off on our pre-flight checks. You inspected the life jackets for tears and checked to be sure that the two 'sparklet' type CO_2 inflator cartridges were there, that they hadn't been pierced and that they were put in the right way. I found life jackets with all these wrong.

They could be blown up manually, if necessary. There was a Sub-machine gun fastened to the wall in the radar compartment. A 'Veery Flare Pistol' and a box of flares were in each plane. These were used for signaling purposes. We never used ours and I can't recall any one else who did. There was a tube about two inches in diameter and a foot long, and this extended through the overhead in the after station. The muzzle of the flare pistol was inserted into this and fired overhead. We carried a piece of vacuum cleaner hose several feet long and when one end was placed out through the flare tube in flight, it became a dandy vacuum cleaner and you could clean up that part of the plane in a hurry. This was very useful because the floor or deck in the after station was made of corrugated aluminum and it was difficult to get clean with other means.

Other than alcohol, I never heard of any kind of drug abuse. I never heard of Marijuana. There was a drawer in the Navigator's table and in the drawer were several Morphine Syrettes. These were intended as a painkiller for wounded crewmen, I never heard of any being used for anything else.

I kept with me and carried from plane to plane, a canvas 'parachute bag'. In this, I kept the charts that I needed, a hand made plastic tuning tool for the radar transmitter, and various assorted tubes and parts, which experience had shown me, might come in handy. Before my tour was over, I had just about everything to fix any fixable problem during our flight patrols. I don't know if I was the best radar operator in the squadron, but I doubt if any one worked more diligently at it. I regularly talked to other operators to see if they had any troubles and what they did about them. On my days off, I talked to ground crew repairmen as to what they had encountered and could they have been fixed in flight. I went to Fleet Headquarters in Tacloban and obtained Hydrographic Charts of our patrol areas. These were superior to the charts we were issued. Was I the only one who did this? Did this make any difference? I don't know but at least it made me feel better.

Our normal bomb load was six-five hundred-pound general-purpose bombs. I think a time or two; planes were loaded with one hundred pound bombs. These were intended for use on airstrips. These made a lot of small craters instead of six big ones. We personally never carried any of these. Why the almost exclusive use of five hundred-pound bombs, I don't know. One thousand-pound bombs were more effective against shipping. With the five hundred pound ones, you had to lay one right up against the side of the ship to be effective. If you put a one thousand pound within fifty yards, it would usually crack the bottom of the ship open.

Those bombs would skip when they hit the surface of the water, just like skipping a flat bottom stone on water. When they dropped from two hundred feet, they stayed right with your plane and first hit the water, almost under the plane. Then they would hop along, losing speed and when fitted with a four-five second delay fuse gave the plane a chance to get clear. Otherwise, if one went off two hundred feet under your plane, it would do as much damage to your plane as the intended target. The pilot normally released the bombs. All the bombardier did was set up the intervalometer to drop the bombs at a selected number of feet apart, if more than one bomb was to be dropped. Experience by previous squadrons had shown that a drop from two hundred feet at two hundred knots was an effective approach. The bombsight we used was primitive, but coupled with experience was effective. The Pitot tube (this gave air-speed information) was plainly visible from the pilot's seat. It was used as the front sight of a pair of open sights. The rear V of the sight (point of aim, like the back sight at the end of a rifle) system was contrived by pasting a V of masking tape to the windshield. Then a run was made on a practice target to see where the bomb had hit. From this, you adjusted the 'rear sight' until you made a direct hit.

Surprisingly, most of the time you could make a free run on a ship, (without being shot at), and bomb them, as their lookouts weren't that alert. A prudent pilot would keep on going, even if your bombs didn't hit the ship. By then you had jarred them awake and if you returned to bomb, they would shoot at you. You left them alone for another day. The pilot could take evasive action on the run going in, but he had to fly that last half-mile in straight and level at two hundred feet and two hundred knots head on.

When we would start our low altitude cross leg, the autopilot would be disengaged and the plane flown manually, but before this was done, the autopilot was set for a level straight ahead climbing flight pattern. Then all you had to do to engage the autopilot, was slap a master switch on. If we got a shell burst in the cockpit that killed or disabled both pilots, who ever could reach that switch, threw it on. This didn't give much of a chance, but it was better than none. As I recall, no one ever had to do this.

The pilot once told us that if we ever had to bail out he would do all he could to control the plane until we were all out. When he said to bail out, he didn't expect any arguments, just leave. I told him that as long as that plane was good enough for him, it was good enough for me. As soon as he bailed out, I would be right behind him. He was not to wait for me to bail out first. The thought of jumping out of an airplane, no matter the circumstances, was

83

something I was least fond of.

Dave, our plane captain, kept bugging the pilot to let him fly the plane. Finally, he got his chance and made a landing at Kaneohe. It wasn't bad, kind of bumpy, but we were down o.k. The pilot wouldn't let him make a take off. Said there was never going to be an occasion when that was necessary and he sure hoped it never came to pass that Dave would have to make a landing. To that I said, 'Amen, Deacon.' "

GLEN EATON

Branch of Service:
   U.S. Navy
Years of Service:
   5 years; 1941 to 1946
Areas Stationed:
   South Pacific
Ships:
   U.S.S. Mascoma (AO83) - Tanker
Specialty:
   "I was the Chief Machinists Mate and worked in the engine room."

"We traveled with the fleet and sometimes went with a destroyer for escort. We fueled the ships with fuel oil and carried diesel fuel. Our decks were loaded with bombs, lubricating oil, and depth charges.

We watched the fleet shelling Iwo Jima. Soon afterwards we went into Tokyo Bay and saw the Japanese when they signed the surrender aboard the U.S.S. Missouri."

HERALD V. ECHOLS

Branch of Service:
U.S. Army (Colonel)
Years of Service:
22 years and 3 months-active service
(26 years and 9 months counting reserve duty)
Outfit:
Branch of Army Ordinance Corps, Armor
Areas Stationed:
Europe, SE Asia, Hawaii, Oregon, California
Specialty:
"My specialty was Armor but due to injuries I was
forced to transfer to the Ordinance Corps where
my injuries would not interfere with my duties."

Lt. Col. H.V. Echols, Battalion Commander,
3rd Ordinance Battalion, Lon Binh, Vietnam
1970 - 1971

"During WWII, I attempted to join a Navy program called the Navy V12 program, but I could not pass the physical exam due to a heart murmur. However, the Merchant Marine offered me a chance to serve my country in a different capacity. At the age of 16, I dropped out of my senior year of high school (which I would never recommend to anyone) and joined the Merchant Marine. I served for 2 years and 3 months as a deck hand aboard two different tankers; the S.S. Mojave and the S.S. Fallen Timbers. I was promoted to Able Bodied Seaman during that time and applied for and was accepted to attend the Merchant Marine Officers Training Academy. When the war ended, I left the Merchant Marine to return to civilian life.

Later I married and went off to college where I received a degree in Civil Engineering and a commission as 2nd Lieutenant in the U.S. Army. While in college I joined the R.O.T.C. (Reserve Officers Training Corps, from which most officers in the military services come from) and an Army Reserve Unit as Private 1st Class in an Armored Troop. I was the troop clerk and was responsible for processing all the troop administrative paper work. I received my 2nd Lieutenant Commission one-year before I graduated, so during my last year in the Reserve Armored Troop I was the troop Commander. It was quite a promotion from Private First Class to 2nd Lieutenant. The reason for this was that the Korean War was on and all the Officers were being called to serve in Korea.

Shortly after graduation from college I was called to active duty to fulfill my R.O.T.C. commitments of serving 2 years active duty.

My first assignment was to Korea with a 3-month stint at Aberdeen Proving Ground in Maryland, to attend officers Basic Training Course. While in training, my orders were changed to an assignment at Augusta Arsenal in Georgia, where I supervised military and civilian employees in the repair and rebuild of military weapons such as pistols, rifles, machine guns, rocket launchers, artillery and anti-aircraft weapons.

I was then re-assigned to the U.S. Army in Europe, the 53rd Ordinance Group, and was responsible for the procuring of ammunition from all the allied countries in Europe and the Middle East.

I traveled all over Europe and the Middle East inspecting the production and testing of the ammunition we purchased. I was also the Headquarters Company Commander (by then I had been promoted to First Lieutenant). On completion of this tour of duty in June of 1957, I was selected for commission as a regular Army Officer. Officers in the Army are categorized in one of two groups; Reserve Officers who serve at the pleasure of the President and can be released at any time, or the Regular Army Officers who serve for a period of 30-years. Presumably, only the best are included as regular Army Officers.

From Europe, I was re-assigned to the 3rd Battalion, 40th Armored Group at Fort Stewart, Georgia and was promoted to Captain and assigned as Company Commander of 'C' Company, 3rd Armored Battalion. After this, I was again assigned to the Officers Advanced Course at Aberdeen Proving Ground. In September of 1960, I joined the U.S. Military Assistance Advisory Group (M.A.A.G.) in Vietnam. I was assigned as an advisor to the 22nd Tank Battalion,

22nd Infantry Division, Army of South Vietnam. I was
stationed at Kon Tum, Vietnam. My duty station was at or
near a village on the Laotian boarder called Dak To, which
literally means 'roads end'. I spent a year advising the
Battalion Commander on how to operate a Tank Battalion.
Dak To was about 40 miles from Kon Tum and a Master
Sergeant and myself were the only Americans there. We
managed to get to Kon Tum about once a month for staff
meetings. We required an armored escort of an infantry
platoon in Armored Personnel Carriers for our safety. While
traveling my Sergeant was killed by a village child who ran
along side our jeep begging for candy while he slipped a
hand grenade behind the driver's seat. The sergeant was
killed as a result, while I miraculously escaped serious
injury.

On completion of my tour of duty in Vietnam, I returned
to the United States and attended Graduate School. I had
several typical peacetime assignments and attended Army
Command and General Staff College.

After an assignment in the office of the Secretary of the
Army, I once more was re-assigned to Vietnam in 1970. I
served one year as the Battalion Commander of the 3rd
Ordnance Battalion. Essentially, I commanded 7 to 12
Ammunition Supply Points (A.S.P.) located throughout
South Vietnam. These A.S.P.'s issued and serviced all the
ammunition used by the U.S. and Vietnamese Army Units
throughout South Vietnam. The Battalion itself consisted of
1,500 officers and men and 250 Vietnamese civilians who
received the ammunition from the ships in Saigon and
hauled it to the depot in Long Binh, where it was stored and
then issued to the A.S.P.'s.

This was by far the largest logistical mission in SE Asia,
and complicated by the fact that it was highly dangerous due

to its explosive nature. It was the one commodity that was absolutely essential to troop survival.

On completion of this tour, I returned to the U.S. where I attended the Armed Forces Industrial College. After completing this course of study, I was assigned to command the Umatilla Army Ordinance Depot in Umatilla, Oregon. I served for one year in Oregon as the Depot Commander. I was promoted to full Colonel and re-assigned as the Commanding Officer of the Department of Defense Contract Administrative Service Office in Los Angeles, California. This job consisted of supervising 540 civilian employees in the purchasing of material for each of the armed services, as well as for NASA. In fact, we supervised the purchase of all the space shuttles for NASA.

Finally, I retired after 22 years and 3 months. I moved to Hermiston, Oregon where I became involved in the construction business. After 17 years in this business, I retired for good.

I give all the credit to God for seeing me safely through my career in the U.S. Army."

Mr. Echols earned many medals during his service to our country:
> Legion of Merit - one oak leaf cluster
> Bronze Star
> Air Medal - one oak leaf cluster
> Army Meritorious Service Medal
> Department of Defense Commendation Medal
> Department of Army Commendation Medal
> Army Service Medal
> Vietnam Service Medal
> Army Expeditionary Medal
> Maritime Pacific Theater Medal

América's True Heroes

Maritime Atlantic Theater Medal
Army Presidential Unit Citation
U.S. Army General Staff Medallion

THOMAS F. ELLIOTT

Branch of Service:
 U.S. Marine Corps   (Corporal)
Years of Service:
 1950 - 1951   Korea
Outfit:
 1st Marine Division
Areas Stationed:
 Throughout South and North Korea
Specialty:
 Shotgun Rider (Motorized Transport)

The following is an article that appeared in
Soldier of Fortune magazine, December 1995,
by Thomas Elliott

The Chosin Few Who Walked on Water

 Dead of winter, 1950. Behind enemy lines, North Korea,
just south of Manchuria at the Chosin Reservoir-cited by
historians as scene of "the most savage battle in modern
warfare," resulting in 17-Medals of Honor and 70-Navy
Crosses awarded, the most for a single battle in U.S. history.
 It was minus 30-degrees Fahrenheit on the frozen waters
of the Chosin Reservoir. Our mission was to locate and
rescue wounded soldiers trapped behind Chinese lines. Our
mission leader was Lieutenant Colonel Olin Beall, USMC,
known as "a tough old bird," even though he did not wear
the eagle of a full colonel. Not a young man, Beall was built
like a bull, strong as an ox, and tenacious as a bulldog.

I first met Beall on the ship carrying us to Korea. He was my C.O. in the 1st Motor Transport Battalion, 1st Marine Division. As C.O., he presided over my court-martial for questioning the ancestry of a young naval officer who queried me regarding general orders when on guard. After some fatherly advice, Beall reduced me a stripe, stipulating I could regain my corporal stripes sometime after reaching our destination.

A month after the amphibious landing at Inchon, we moved into North Korea. Our movement northward through the mountains of North Korea came to a halt when 15,000, Marines and 4,000, soldiers were surrounded. The 80-mile route to the sea was severed by 120,000, ChiCom soldiers.

Hagaru-ri was the central hub for U.S. forces, containing logistics for a sustained drive toward China. On the right flank, east of the Chosin Reservoir, two Army regiments (31st and 32nd of 7th Division), were advancing along a narrow dirt road parallel to the reservoir. On the left flank, two Marine regiments (5th and 7th Marines) were in the mountainous region near the hamlet of Yodamni. When Chinese forces poured from the hills, both Army and Marine units had to fight their way back to Hagaru. After several days of intense fighting, the Marines returned as an organized fighting force, but the Army was clobbered in the open and defenseless terrain east of the Chosin.

On the defensive perimeter at Hagaru, the sector assigned to B Company faced north across the barren reservoir. Truck drivers and mechanics lay in the snow for eight hours. On the other side of the perimeter, the silence was occasionally broken by water-cooled machine guns as gunners fired to keep them from freezing.

With word of possible friendlies infiltrating our lines, flares were fired and we saw ghost-like movement on the ice as hundreds of soldiers approached. Some were limping, some crawled, and others were carrying or dragging their buddies. As they passed through our line, most were crying and thanking God for their deliverance. None had expected to see Marines holding Hagaru; they feared we had pulled out south-and that by morning all would be massacred.

Beall learned from Army survivors that additional wounded were along the east bank, and from Marine aviators that the Army truck convoy stretched more than four miles. The skipper asked for volunteers.

Moving out slowly with jeeps, trailers, blankets and medical supplies, a dozen of us went up the middle of the reservoir. After an eternity of freezing hell, we came to the burned-out convoy. Hills overlooking the road were honeycombed with Chinese positions. The ice was covered by snow, and thin puffs of white told us they were trying to get our range. Knowing the Chinese were watching through binoculars, Beall had us lay our weapons slowly on the hoods of the jeeps. He ordered two men to pick up their rifles and follow him to the shoreline. Beall did not carry a rifle himself.

Leaving the riflemen at the shoreline, Beall inspected the trucks, sending the walking wounded to the jeeps. Those who could not walk were carried. One soldier was so badly shot up; Beall hoisted him over his shoulder and carried him himself. The long walk back to Hagaru was uneventful except other stragglers, all wounded or half-frozen, were picked up along the way. A second trip was made by Beall that afternoon when spotter planes saw other groups of men by the shore.

Of the 2,500, Army troops east of the Chosin, only 1,050, survived-319 of which are credited to Beall and his drivers. A week later, fighting through what seemed like half the population of China, we reached the sea and the transports to carry us south, to fight another day.

Aboard ship, 5,000 men jammed into compartments for 2,500. Searching the ship for a place to stash my gear, I reached the upper decks and "Officer Country." The sign read, "Officer Shower Room, Crew Only." It was empty. I grabbed the opportunity for a quick wash and shave. Stripping to my skivvies, I stashed my gear in a lifeboat. After 10-minutes of hot soapy water, the door burst open and two-field grade Marine Officers entered: One was Lt. Col. Beall. It was time to accept the consequences, so I stepped out from behind the curtain.

"Good morning, Colonel," I said.

"Good morning, Lieutenant, good to see you survived the trip down the mountain!" Beall commented, with a twinkle.

"Yes, sir," I responded.

"Come by my headquarters when we get to our destination. I want to discuss that young man under your command and his promotion to Corporal."

A week later, true to his word, Beall sent down the paperwork returning my "lost" stripe.

Each year, members of B Company, 1st MTB, 1st MarDiv, gather in San Diego. The weeklong festivity is solemnized by a visit to Fort Rosecrans Military Cemetery. At the grave of Lt. Col. Olin Beall, silent prayers are said over our hero-not only a great warrior and humanitarian, but "a tough old bird," who did indeed, walk on water.

The next article appeared in <u>Leatherneck</u> magazine, June 2001
by Thomas Elliott

Letter of the Month

I experienced a trip to Korea in 1975, on the war's 25th anniversary, when my wife, Dolores, and I journeyed to Seoul, Inchon, and Panmunjom.

Several bus loads of Korean War veterans and their wives left the hotel in Seoul for a day visit to Inchon. Before returning to Seoul, the buses stopped at a shopping mall in Yongdong-Po, where the ladies of our group attacked the shops with credit cards in hand.

I was wearing a baseball cap with "U.S. Marines" across the front. In addition, I had attached a large gold Marine emblem. A small crowd of Korean women and children gathered about to watch the American tourists. One nice-looking, young Korean woman had an older "mama-san" with her, and they kept pointing to my cap, then pointing to my feet.

I asked the bus driver, who spoke English well, to interpret. The young lady, who also spoke excellent English, explained that her grandmother called me "yellow legs." It then dawned on me that back in 1950, when Marines came ashore at Inchon, then on to take Seoul, little children would dance around, pointing to our mustard-colored leggings. The kids had all been exposed for five years to the U.S. Army occupational troops with their spit-shined combat boots, and now the children would sing, "Boots, no-yellow legs, yes-number one!" It seems that the leggings had become our badge of honor.

The young Korean woman then asked if her grandmother

could speak to me. She explained that her grandmother knew only a few English words. The mama-san hesitated a moment, then approached me, laid her hand on my arm, looked into my eyes and said, "Thank you."

Those were the most beautiful words I have ever heard, and because they came from the heart, it brought tears to my eyes and a lump to my throat, for I knew she was saying the words for every Marine, soldier, sailor and airman who had come to her country so many years ago.

LAWRENCE D. FAIRBAIRN

Branch of Service:
   U.S. Navy (Sea Bees)
Years of Service:
   24 years
   Liberation of the Island of Guam 7/21/1944.
   Korean War 1952 - Summer-Fall Offensive
   Vietnam War 1/1964 - 7/1964 and 4/1966 - 6/1966
Outfit:
   25th Construction Battalion
   Amphibious Construction Battalion #1
   3rd Mobile Construction Battalion
Areas Stationed:
   South Pacific, Korea, South Vietnam
Specialty:
   Heavy Equipment Operation

"I was a small part of an offensive operation against a determined enemy and the liberation of native people of Guam. It is quite difficult to put into words what I experienced during combat operations. My wartime duty was with the 3rd Marine Division during the operation on Guam and the 1st Marine Division in Vietnam. My unit during the Korean War was assigned to the 8th Army.

I feel that in peacetime the experience I had while assigned to the South Pole Station in Antarctica (1959 -1960) was very noteworthy. It was a learning experience in extreme cold weather operations. I also had the opportunity to serve with the Russian Trans-Antarctic Expedition."

WILLIAM FENTON

Branch of Service:
> U.S. Navy

Years of Service:
> 2 tours in Korea and China (9 years total service)

Areas Stationed:
> San Diego, California; Astoria, Oregon; Sand Point, Washington

Ships or Aircraft:
> U.S.S. Philippine Sea CV47
> AD Sky Raider
> Planeview (an experimental high speed hydrofoil-
> information now unclassified)

Specialty:
> "I worked as a Pipe Fitter, Flight Deck Repairman, did damage control and carried a B.A.R. for our landing parties. I taught Counter Espionage, Fire Fighting and Oceanographic Research. On shore, I was a procurer of specialty parts for the ship and aircrew"

"It was one great rush. I learned that team work is what it is all about, and you need all the information and education you can get on what ever you are doing. Korea made me understand how important life is."

Mr. Fenton just last year (2004) received 2 medals that he earned serving in the Korean War. They were presented to him by a 2 star General at Fort Lewis, Washington.

Nicholas Rider and William Fenton at Civil Air Patrol, February 2006

ALAN E. FERRINGTON

Branch of Service:
U.S. Navy
Years of Service:
2 years, 4 months
Areas Stationed:
South Pacific
Ships:
U.S.S. West Virginia
Specialty:
Medical Corpsman

"I enlisted in the Navy on September 15, 1943. At that stage of the war, Washington had decided to stop all enlistments and let the draft system select and place personnel where they felt the people were needed most. So one had to volunteer to be drafted and then choose the branch of service they desired. I had passed the Navy test for officers training (V12) program but since my high school grades were not as good as they could have been, they passed me by. There were too many wartime distractions, and the fact that I worked the night shift at the local hospital did not help my academic endeavors.

I went through basic training at the Great Lakes Naval Training Station and attended the Navy Indoctrination School at Great Lakes. The Naval Indoctrination School was set up for people who had previous medical experience. The Navy wanted to show us how to do it the 'Navy way'. The people in the class were pharmacists, opticians, chiropractors, and any other medical personnel. We even had two registered male nurses (the Army and Navy gave commissions to female RN's, but male nurses were enlisted men). This was a little reverse discrimination I would say.

After finishing the Indoctrination School, I was placed on a staff of the hospital at Great Lakes while awaiting assignment. After about two months of this duty, I was ordered to Camp Shoemaker in California. This was a staging area in the Central California Valley. From this base people were sent either to the fleet or to some base on the West Coast or Hawaii. The average stay there was about 4-days. I received my orders to go to Bremerton to join the fleet on the West Virginia.

The West Virginia was sunk during the Pearl Harbor attack, December 7, 1941. She was raised, patched up and towed to Bremerton from Hawaii. This must have been a very interesting experience for the people on that sea-going tug! Japanese submarines were patrolling the Pacific and especially the West Coast. I spoke to one of the yard workers who worked on our ship during the patching stage. He said that they patched some holes with sheet steel and other holes were filled with cement (to be removed later).

The ship was virtually rebuilt from the hull up. The superstructure was modified and the latest in 5-inch guns and fire control equipment was installed. Fire control in Navy talk does not pertain to putting out fires, but to control the shooting of the big guns.

We had our shake down off the California coast near San Clemente Island. We shot at targets on a small Island near San Clemente, and also shot at drones and other targets. The shake down was uneventful except for one accident. The newest fire control designed by G.E. caused a shell to go off in the breach. The civilian engineers from G.E. were still on board so we had immediate attention to this problem.

We had a repair ship come alongside at Long Beach to repair and replace any suspicious gun parts.

We then went on to Pearl Harbor to discharge any passengers and take on fuel and other supplies. After a week in Pearl Harbor, we left for the South Pacific. On our way to our assigned area, we crossed the Equator and the International Dateline at the same time. We had a ritual initiation for all hands who had never crossed before, and it was given rather sadistically by the shellback who had been there before. The officers were singled out more judiciously than the enlisted people were.

We arrived at Manus in the Admiralty Islands. It is almost on the Equator and very hot. This was another staging area for the fleet. In this large, natural harbor, we saw every type of ship imaginable. Since this was wartime, every scow that could carry supplies was pressed into service. There were ships from many different nations, and supply depots were set up on the beach. We had our mail and supplies brought on board and some liberty was given the crew. Because the Island was a jungle loaded with mosquitoes, the Army had planes spraying the jungles almost every day. A few Japanese were still holding out in the hills and the Army told us that they found some of the Japs sneaking into the chow lines because they were starving.

We went to the Philippine Islands and shelled the beach at Leyte so the Army and Marines could go ashore. We stood offshore just incase the Japanese Air Force attacked. They still had many airfields on the Islands. During this time, a Japanese Torpedo Bomber came in and torpedoed the cruiser Honolulu. We were sent along the coast to shell any targets on land. Some Jap tanks were spotted and just as we started shooting our five-inch guns, we felt a bump.

We had run aground. The harbor had not been charted in several years so we were not certain of the water depths. We reversed and were free!

The next day we were alerted that a large Japanese force of big ships was coming our way. We made all preparations for a big battle. That night we were summoned to general quarters and informed that the Japanese forces were coming across the Suragao Straits. Their plan was to wipe out the beachhead that we had established at Leyte. We had the advantage because the Japanese had to come up a narrow strait and we could set ourselves broadside. This meant we were going to cross our enemies T. This is a classic naval maneuver and every naval officer dreams of such an opportunity.

We let the P.T. boats go in first (this is the action where John Kennedy had his problem). When they had shot their torpedoes and were clear, we opened fire. Included in this engagement were several of the old battleships, cruisers and destroyers, a sort of the used car fleet in action. We fired our armor piercing 16-inch shells repeatedly. Then the shooting stopped and we were informed that our fleet had destroyed this part of the Japanese Navy. We had expended most of our armor piercing shells. Our guns had metal protruding about 2-inches from the barrels from all the firing. We were riding about 5-inches higher in the water from the loss of so much weight. We then returned to Leyte.

At Leyte, we were given liberty. We saw the country we had been shelling. Crude houses with pigs and water buffalo roaming the streets.

That night, we had another general quarters and this time it was to inform us of a new problem. A huge Japanese force was seen coming down the east side of the Islands. This force we were told had the biggest and best of Japanese battleships and carriers. We were low on fuel and low on armor piercing shells, but we had some shells used for shore engagements left. So our ship, two other old battleships, cruisers, and destroyers set out to intercept this fleet. Their intention was to wipe out the landing forces on Leyte. (At this stage, MacArthur was nowhere in sight). Our attitude was that this was going to be one heck of a fight. After cruising for several hours, we were again called to general quarters. We thought that this was it. However, we were told that the Japanese had been routed by the carriers of Halsey's fleet. After we found out that this was not the case, Halsey had disappeared chasing a ruse fleet, giving rise to the famous radiogram; "Halsey, where are you, the world wonders?"

We found out later that a small task force consisting of baby flat tops (aircraft carriers made from would be merchant ships), and destroyers intercepted the Japanese. This force fought well and did some damage to the smaller Japanese ships. In the confusion of the battle, the Japanese thought that they had encountered Halsey's fleet with big carriers and fast cruisers. They did a 180-degree turn and fled the scene. Ironically, later in the war Halsey's fleet of carriers did find these ships and sunk them.

After this battle, and the scare of the eastern Philippine area, we were sent on duty to shell enemy emplacements any place in the area. We were subject to many air attacks some were Kamikazes. The baby flat top working next to us was hit and sunk and we picked up many survivors. The name of the carrier was Linguean Gulf. We continued up to the harbor near Manila and did some patrolling. We then received an order to proceed to New Hebrides at Esperito Santos. It seems that when we ran aground we did damage to the screws. This port had a floating dry-dock where repairs could be made so we went to this group of Islands. A beautiful spot, virtually untouched by the war. No civilian activities there so liberties were limited to swimming on the beautiful beaches.

We were then ordered to go to Iwo Jima. It seems that the very old battleship New York had lost a screw. We were to replace her and give the Marines gun power to knock out the Japanese emplacements and perform other fire duties as required. We worked in close to the pile of cinders and did what the Marines wanted. We strafed with our 40mm guns, a little out cropping of rocks where the Japanese had a machine gun stationed.

After the shooting at Suriago Straits, we went to a place called Keramo Rhetto to replace our depleted ammunition supply. This was a group of rocks set in the ocean with a natural harbor in the middle. It made one think of paintings by Salvador Dali.

Our orders were now to go to Okinawa and do some more shooting. Kamikazes were attacking quite often. We gave fire support to various spots on the Islands. We also bombarded Shiri Castle. An old castle with walls that were very thick. We were told that the shells bounced off the thick walls but the concussion had killed all the Japanese inside. When Marines came to take it, they found the Japanese all dead. We stayed at Okinawa for some time, fighting off Japanese aircraft and spotting for the Army and Marines. The Kamikazes were very thick and three of them hit us.

Just before the war ended, we were told that we were going to Formosa to set up a staging area for the invasion of Japan. The Atomic Bomb ended that plan. We were still in Okinawa when the war was ended. The Army on shore started firing so we thought we were being attacked. It was only some crazy soldiers who let loose with big guns.

On to Japan...We were asked to go to the homeland of war and keep order in case of any insurgent action. As we approached the Islands, we saw many Japanese ships (both civilian and naval) with their flags drooping in the routine of surrender. As we entered the harbor of Tokyo, we were boarded by a Japanese Pilot. He was so short that we had to get an apple box for him to stand on to guide us into the harbor."

DEAN FINLEY

Branch of Service:
   U.S. Navy
Years of Service:
   1948-1955
Outfit:
   Fleet air Wing 14 (1949 - 1951)
   Naval Air Training Command (1951 - 1953)
   Fighter Squadron 141 (1953 - 1955)
Areas Stationed:
   NAS North Island, Pensacola, Florida; Kingsville,
   Texas; Miramar, California
Ships:
   U.S.S. Randolph and U.S.S. Hancock
Specialty:
   Naval Aviator

   "I was a test pilot for project steam on the U.S.S. Hancock
in October 1954. This project involved testing the new (at
the time) steam catapults and constant run-out arresting
gear."

ARTHUR W. FRENZEL

Branch of Service:
> U.S. Army and U.S. Coast Guard

Years of Service:
> 32 (active and reserve combined)

Outfit:
> 456th Ordinance Company

Areas Stationed:
> Tucson, AZ; March field, CA; Muroc, Dry lakes, CA;
> Hatbox Field, Muskogee, OK; Brady, TX; Lubbock, TX;
> Hondo, TX; Hobbs, NM; Roswell, NM; Lincoln, NA

Aircraft:
> B-13, AT-9, AT-17, AT-7, C-47, C-60, B-25, B-29, B-17

Specialty:
> Pilot and Supply Officer

"I enlisted in the U.S. Army in June 1941, and was assigned to the 456th Ordnance Company in Tucson Arizona. Their function was to supply explosive ordinance to the B-18 Army Bombers. We were on maneuvers December 7, 1941, at March Field, California and had the opportunity to visit my parents in Los Angeles. As a friend and I were driving my parent's auto, we heard on the radio the report of the Japanese bombing Pearl Harbor, Hawaii. Quickly we returned to March Field where we prepared to go to Muroc, Dry Lakes, California to establish a supply base for our ordinance. The opportunity opened for pilot training in the Army Air Corps. I had already soloed a small plane the previous year so I applied and was accepted as an 'Avian Student' I was not an Avian Cadet because I had no college degree. Instructions and flying were the same. Preliminary flight school was at Hatbox Field, Muskogee, Oklahoma and basic training was at Brady, Texas where we flew B13's. We moved on to twin engine advanced training at Lubbock, Texas flying AT-9 and AT-17. We graduated as Staff Sergeant Pilots in September of 1942, as Class 42-I. My dear mother was there to pin on my wings. As a pilot, I was assigned to Army Air Corp Navigation School (AACNS) at Hondo, Texas. For two years, we had the opportunity to fly AT-7, C-47, C-60, and B-25's that were temporarily assigned to the field. I also had the additional duty as Supply Officer. In 1944, I was promoted to the new rank of Flight Officer, and assigned to a B-17 school in Hobbs, New Mexico. I received a new commission rank of 2nd Lieutenant and was able to obtain lead Pilot rating. Early 1945, I went to Lincoln, Nebraska to form a lead crew. We were awaiting orders to go to Okinawa or vicinity when the Japanese surrendered. I had accrued enough discharge points and was ordered to return to Fort Mac Arthur, California for an honorable discharge.

As a banker prior to military service, I returned to banking, retained my reserve commission and transferred to the California Air National Guard. In order to retain flying proficiency I attempted to fly the Guards AT-6 aircraft, but was only successful in obtaining 8 hours over the next 2 years. This was not enough to enable proficiency in flying, although I did obtain a promotion to 1st Lieutenant. Around 1949, a friend who was a commander in the U.S. Coast Guard tempted me to a testing and transfer to the Coast Guard. This was successful and I transferred to the U.S. Coast Guard Reserve as a Lieutenant J.G. on a non-flying basis. Years of enjoyable service, promotion through Lieutenant Commander and retirement from the activities of port security and Merchant Marine Inspection, led to leaving the military services after 32 years, both active duty and reserve duty. I have been proud to serve in the military services of the greatest nation on earth."

Joseph F. Frye

Branch of Service:
   U.S. Marine Corps
Years of Service:
   "I served from 1962 through 1976. I was in while the
   Bay of Pigs was going on in Cuba. My outfit, the 7th
   Engineer Battalion, was put on stand by, but we didn't
   have to go aboard ship. I served two tours of duty in
   Vietnam."
Outfit:
   7th Engineer Battalion
   "B" Company, 3rd Shore Party Battalion
   FLSG "B"
   2nd LAMS Battalion
Areas Stationed:
   Marine Corps Recruit Depot San Diego, California
   (Boot Camp); Camp Pendleton, California; Marine
   Corps Air Station, Hawaii; Vietnam; Okinawa;
   Marine Corps Recruit Depot Paris Island, South
   Carolina; Marine Corps Cold Weather Training
   Center Bridgeport, California; Marine Corps Air
   Station Yuma, Arizona
Ships:
   "I was not stationed aboard a ship, but spent a lot of
   time on one. I went to Hawaii by ship and we went to
   Vietnam by ship. My outfit took Battalions and landed
   them in Vietnam by ship."
Specialty:
   Heavy Equipment Operator

"I remember being enlisted by a First Sergeant by the name of Davis. He told me at the time that I was about to have an experience that I would not want to go through again for a million dollars, but at the same time, I would not take a million dollars for the experience. Being an 18-year old, I had no idea how true this would be.

I had no idea I was joining a group that would have a bond that would last a lifetime. When you hear the saying, 'a band of brothers,' this is so true of the Marines. By being a Marine, you are a brother to all Marines. We ate, slept, laughed, cried, and at times saw our friends get killed, but we always remained strong for our fellow Marines.

The experience of Vietnam had a huge effect on me. I had good experiences as well as bad. I think we must learn from these experiences and make changes for the better from them. I am so happy to see that we as a nation have learned a valuable lesson from Vietnam in the way we treat and care for the troops now in Iraq.

One of the experiences I had in Vietnam was going in around April of 1965. We landed and off loaded in a park at the University of Hue, in Hue City. It is located on the Perfume River. We spent one-month there and then went on to build a base at Phu-Bi.

I was back in Hue City in 1968, during the Tet offensive. The University of Hue was one of the areas that were heaviest hit with fighting. I was able to see the city before the destruction and after. I can remember thinking it was one of the more beautiful spots in Vietnam before Tet.

During the time we were building the base at Phu-Bi, I met a Vietnamese family living near the airstrip. There was a little girl around the age of 11 or 12, and a boy named Coo who was around 8 or 9. One day, I realized the girl would go to school, and the next day the boy would go. I asked Coo

one day why this was, and he told me his family only had
enough money for one of them to go to school, so they took
turns. I asked him how much it cost to go, and he told me
$.30 a day. At that time, I told him if he would go everyday I
would give him the $.30. I remember each day when he
came home he would find me and show me his work from
school. The one thing I wish is that I could have found out
how things turned out for him.

As I look back over my time spent in the service, I do not
have any regrets. I had some good times and became
acquainted with a lot of good people, some I am still in
contact with today."

(left to right) Tom Baum, Dave Traylor and Joseph Frye, dedicating a paved park
trail and bench to their buddy, Jimmy Allen, who was in Vietnam with them.
June 2005

114

JOSE DE LA LUIZ GARCIA

Branch of Service:
    U.S. Navy
Years of Service:
    4 years - WWII
Areas Stationed:
    San Diego, California (boot camp); Astoria, Oregon
Ships:
    U.S.S. Lenawee APA 195
Specialty:
    Mr. Garcia was part of the boat crew on a landing
    barge that transported the soldiers to the beach.

Mr. Garcia toured many areas of the Pacific during his tour of duty: Okinawa, Ulithi, New Hebrides, Solomon Islands, Guam, Iwo Jima, Saipan, Hawaiian Islands (Pearl Harbor), Tokyo and the Philippines.

Mr. Garcia witnessed the raising of the flag on Iwo Jima. He was also present in Tokyo Bay on September 2, 1945, the day of the official surrender of the Japanese Empire and the close of World War II.

Mr. Garcia earned two stars for the Asiatic-Pacific Area, the Philippine Liberation and the Victory Medal for WWII.

CHARLES F. GLADISH

Branch of Service:
    U.S. Air Force
Years of Service:
    8 years
Outfit:
    23rd Tactical Fighter Squadron,
    36th Tactical Fighter Wing
Areas Stationed:
    Bitburg, Germany and Nellis AFB, Nevada
Aircraft:
    F-100 and F-105
Specialty:
    Fighter/Bomber, Nuclear Weapons Delivery

"I was stationed in Bitburg, Germany from 1960 to 1963, during the initial building of the Berlin Wall. I began instructing in the F-105 at Nellis AFB, Nevada from 1963 to 1966. I joined the Pan American World Airways in 1966, and returned to Berlin, Germany in 1987. I witnessed the destruction of the Berlin Wall (as a civilian) in 1989."

MARION "BOB" GRAY

Branch of Service:
U.S. Army (SSgt.)
Years of Service:
1943 - 1945   WWII
Outfit:
Company K, 9th Infantry Regiment (Manchu),
2nd Infantry Division
Areas Stationed:
Landed D-Day, June 6, 1944, Dog Green Sector,
Omaha Beach
Battle of the Bulge; Belgium, Germany
Specialty:
Infantryman

SSgt. Marion "Bob" Gray joined the Army Air Corps and
was transferred to the 9th Infantry Regiment in 1943. He
graduated from Expert Infantry Training at Camp Bullis,
Texas. In 1944, he was sent to Wales where he joined the
9th Infantry, Company K. Just before the Invasion of
France, he was sent to the Assault Training Center in
Staunton Sands, England. The men were highly guarded,
were not allowed to leave the compound and were asked to
remove their patches and rank. Two days later they boarded
trains to a hanger sized building where they were issued
their gear.

On June 6, SSgt. Gray and 150 other 2nd Division soldiers
in their special engineer task force boarded a ship to cross
the English Channel heading for Dog Green Sector on
Omaha Beach. Their objective was to blow up Nazi obstacles
on the beach. One mile off shore, they boarded a LCM

loaded with soldiers, wooden boxes, canisters, and primer coils. A Lieutenant was instructing the men to keep moving, don't stop, push ahead, do not stop to help anyone, and keep moving forward.

Leaving the LCM, SSgt. Gray sank in about eight feet of water. He skillfully used his rifle to get himself back up to the surface for air, and then would sink down again. As he fought his way to shore, SSgt. Gray spotted a wounded soldier and tried to drag him to shore. He lost his grip on him just as the soldier was hit in the shoulder and neck. The beach was covered with bodies, gear, and debris. There was intense enemy gunfire constantly coming from the overhead cliffs. Most of the men who left the same LCM as SSgt. Gray, either drowned or were killed and never made it to the beach.

On the shore, SSgt. Gray threw away his sand filled rifle and picked up one from a dead G.I. He frantically ran to the base of the cliff where he spent most of the day alone. It was not until evening that he climbed up a low area of the cliff and started inland. In the dark, he met up with a frightened First Lieutenant from the First Infantry Division. Between the two of them, they figured they were close to Vierville-sur -mer. They spent a sleepless night in a ditch, and the next morning, located part of the Lieutenant's unit. SSgt. Gray decided to sew his 2nd Division patch back on hoping someone would recognize it and be able to tell him the location of his unit. Although, it was three more days before SSgt. Gray located members of his Second Division.

On December 18, 1944, (Day 2 of the Battle of the Bulge), SSgt. Gray's Company K was captured at the Lausdell farmhouse, near the twin villages of Krinkelt-Rocherath in Belgium. Twelve soldiers were not captured and SSgt. Gray was one of them. He led the survivors and about seventy other soldiers, four and a half miles to the safety of Elsenborn Ridge in Belgium.

For a short time before being transferred to the Battery B-155, Cannon Crew, SSgt. Gray worked with the Graves Registration. This was an outfit assigned to identify the dead, locate any known positions of dead soldiers, and bury the remains in a temporary cemetery. Sometimes the "buddies" of a fallen soldier would try to identify on a map where a soldier laid. Deep snow would often prevent immediate recovery of the remains. Therefore, many soldiers remain "Missing in Action" because no identifiable remains were ever found.

FRANK G. GROSS

Branch of Service:
> U.S. Marine Corps

Years of Service:
> 3 years (4 months Combat)   Korean War

Outfit:
> 1st Division, Item Company, 3rd Battalion

Areas Stationed:
> Parris Island, South Carolina; Camp Lejeune, North Carolina; Good Will Occupation-Europe

Ships:
> U.S.S. Salem (LST980)

Specialty:
> Rifleman, B.A.R. (in Combat)

"While on duty in Turkey, we were shipped up the Suez Canal to make a landing in Inchon, Korea. We went on to liberate Seoul, Korea and then we went up to the Frozen Chosin, where I was seriously injured with frostbite. I was sent back to the States, and spent eleven months in the Philadelphia Naval Hospital.

It was there, on December 29, 1950, that I composed 'The Ballad of Chosin'. This composition is on my album and CD, along with seven ballads of honor. The CD is titled: 'Ballads of Honor Korea'. It is now in process of promotion to a D.V.D."

JOHN E. GROVES

Branch of Service:
U.S. Air Force
Years of Service:
1968 - 1972   Vietnam
Outfit:
22nd Tactical Reconnaissance Squadron
Areas Stationed:
Mountain Home AFB, Idaho
Shaw AFB, South Carolina
Specialty:
Aircraft Maintenance (Crew Chief)

"I took basic training at Lackland AFB in San Antonio, Texas, and tech school at Shepard AFB in Wichita Falls, Texas. My first assignment with the 22nd TRS was at Mountain Home AFB in Idaho. This was a training base for the F4 Phantom pilots and personnel that were headed for overseas assignments. In late 1970, we moved the 22nd TRS to Shaw AFB in Sumpter, South Carolina, where we continued to train personnel. I was discharged in 1972."

George E. Hall

Branch of Service:
U.S. Army
Years of Service:
18 months   WWII
Outfit:
516th M.P. Battalion
Areas Stationed:
Heidelberg, Allen, Frankfort; Germany
Fort Bliss, Camp Wheeler; U.S.A.
Specialty:
"No specialty, I just did what ever duty our outfit was assigned to do."

"Arriving in Germany during the 'Battle of the Bulge', I was assigned to the Seventh Army, 516th M.P. Battalion. I was still in a state of turmoil over the unthinkable death of my baby. She was just 90-days old. Those lonely and trying nights became one horrible and continuous nightmare. Always my little Ella would appear, her tiny arms reaching out to me. Battling against an unseen power, I could never get quite close enough to touch her. At that point, my strength was completely exhausted. Such torture can only be called hell on earth. Always, I wound up screaming or sobbing until shaken awake by one of my comrades.

Then one day along the Rhine River, I had to take a small child from the arms of her father-one of Hitler's despised elite S.S. troopers. As I reached for her, baby Ella and the horrible nightmare, came crashing into my mind. Although, the S.S. were said to be void of all emotion, at his little girl's cry of "Papa! Papa!" tears slid down that S.S. trooper's face, the same as mine. Time seemed to stop. For a few brief moments, we were no longer soldiers and enemies, just two fathers torn with grief. Yet, we both knew it could not last, that I must carry out my duty.

Breaking the grip of that innocent little war victim and forcefully pulling her from her father was one of the hardest things I ever had to do. Her frightened cries of "Papa! Papa!" still rings in my ears. Pretending she was my little Ella, I briefly held her close to my heart and said, "Ich liebe dich kinder." (I love you little one). Then handing her to her weeping mother, I escorted my prisoner to a waiting vehicle."

"The end of the war scene before us was unexpected, yet they were there-the young, the old, the defeated, the disfigured and destitute. Interspersed amid the rubble, they crowded into every available space along the city streets. The final big one, the 'Battle of the Bulge', was now history! Their country lay in ashes. The one exception was the city of Heidelberg.

Our outfit, the 516th M.P. Battalion, was in the town of Worms, Germany. Hour after hour, we were marched up and down the streets. I guess it was to show the enemy we still had plenty of able-bodied troops. So here we were, victor and vanquished, looking at one another. I still see those faces staring at us. No words were spoken nor were they needed. One could see and feel the myriad of emotions-gladness, hatred, confusion, pain, hunger, and possible death.

Seeing such a mass of destruction and despair, my heart called for compassion. However, my head said, they are the enemy; but for them you would not be here.

Later, on a cold and snowy morning in Heidelberg, war-

124

weary and longing for home, I was on traffic duty. Suddenly, I saw a jeep approaching at a high rate of speed. I automatically glanced to where some children were playing. To my horror, a little girl possibly three-years of age was sitting in the street. I quickly motioned the driver to slow down. Rather than using his gears, he set the brakes, which sent the jeep skidding right toward the helpless little child. I knew her life was in my hands. Dashing to her side, I grabbed her arm, spun her across the snow-packed road, leaped into the air and landed, uninjured, on the hood of the jeep.

I take no credit for such a feat. It was God's power, not mine. God chose to perform a miracle by increasing this soldier boy's ability that he might save a precious little life."

At age 80, Mr. Hall decided to celebrate his birthday by hiking the Apache Indian trail from the East Stronghold over the Dragoon Mountains, to the West Stronghold and back. This is a ten-mile hike and is 1,900-feet in altitude. He has continued to hike it every year on his birthday. Mr. Hall is now 85.

JAMES HAMPTON

Branch of Service:
U.S. Navy Reserve
Years of Service:
1941 - 1945 WWII
Outfit:
VF-2 Fighter squadron II, later assigned to VF-11
Fighter Squadron
Areas Stationed:
Pacific Ocean
Ships:
U.S.S. Lexington and U.S.S. Hornet (aircraft carriers)
Specialty:
Aircraft mechanic on F4F aircraft. "When I was
Discharged I had the rank of Aviation Machinist Mate
First Class Petty Officer."

Mr. Hampton served on aircraft carriers during the Second World War. The large carriers held over 3,000 men. They consisted of the men who ran the ship and the men who flew and took care of the aircraft based on the ship. There were three types of aircraft on the carriers; fighter planes used for fighting enemy planes, dive-bombers and the planes that carried torpedoes, which were released from the plane into the water to blow up other ships. All aircraft had combustion engines because jet planes were not used during WWII. The top deck of the carrier was the flight deck where the planes took off and landed. A huge cable stretched across the deck to catch the planes on landing. The planes were repaired and stored on the hanger deck, which was located right below the flight deck. An elevator was used to move planes from one deck to the other. The planes wings were folded up over their fuselage for storage.

During the Battle of Coral Sea, May 1942, the Japanese had plans to attack Australia. Our ships stopped the plan by sinking the Japanese light carrier Shoho and badly damaging the heavy aircraft carrier Shokaku. The Lexington was in turn attacked by the Japanese and received many torpedo bomb hits. After several hours of repairs being made to the ship, the Captain decided to move the ship. When it moved, the fuel lines ruptured and fires broke out. The carrier stored many gallons of fuel for the planes, so when the fires broke out the fuel made fighting those fires much more difficult. The ship's Commander realized he had no choice but to order abandon ship. At this time, all airplanes had to be abandoned and shoved over the side of the ship into the water. Mr. Hampton's squad had to wait on the upper deck for their order to abandon ship. They were told to remove their shoes so they would not be hindered with the heavy shoes filled with water when trying

127

to swim. Someone remembered some ice cream in the galley down on the lower decks. The smallest man was sent over the side, through a hole torn in the side of the ship near the galley. He was able to bring all the ice cream he could carry back to the men waiting above. Soon after finishing the ice cream, they received their orders to go overboard. They did not leap into the water, but threw ropes over the side and climbed down. The life rafts that were assigned to the aircraft were inflated and held several men. Others held onto rings attached to the raft. Then a launch (large motorboat) from another ship arrived to pick up the men. Other American ships circled the stricken ship to help pick up survivors. Mr. Hampton was taken to the cruiser U.S.S. New Orleans. There he met a man from his hometown who gave him clothing to wear, and let him sleep in his bunk. His friend's shoes were two sizes too large, but he was grateful to have them. The "Lex" refused to sink, so after everyone was safely away, our ships sunk it with several torpedoes.

After this experience with the U.S.S. Lexington Mr.Hampton was stationed for a while in the States. At one time, his outfit was supposed to be assigned to another carrier, but then ended up on Guadalcanal.

By the time, Mr. Hampton arrived on the island most of the Japanese had been cleared out. Although, the men had to be very cautious of straggler enemy snipers hiding in trees and the jungle areas around the planes they were assigned to work on.

There were supply problems at times and their food did not always reach them. They were forced to eat food left by the Japanese. Mr. Hampton remembers losing weight because the food at times consisted only of rice loaded with weevils.

Mr. Hampton was next assigned to the U.S.S. Hornet. This trip sent them near the island of Japan itself. They had many encounters with the enemy. They made attacks on Japan and the Philippines and sank many Japanese ships.

Eventually, the crew returned to the states and Mr. Hampton spent the remainder of the war at an airbase in Pasco, Washington.

VERA HAMPTON (HENDRICKS)

Branch of Service:
U.S. Navy Reserves; WAVES (Women Accepted for Volunteer Emergency Service)

Years of Service:
Enlisted April 30, 1944; Discharged April 1946

Areas Stationed:
Boot Camp: New York City, New York (6 weeks)
Yeoman School: Stillwater, Oklahoma
U.S. Naval Supply Depot: Oakland, California

Specialty:
Yeoman

Mrs. Hampton's duties in the WAVES were clerical duties, which consisted of typing, filing etc. Her building supplied the ships in the Pacific with food. Mrs. Hampton typed up the invoices that charged the ships for the food supplied to them. Her outfit also supplied gifts and extra things the sailors used while on board a ship.

The Navy WAVES played a critical roll in the war effort. Both the Navy WAVE and the Army WACS (Women's Army Corps) performed various duties from clerks, to mechanics, to working in hospitals. Regardless of their duties, they were there to replace the men stateside, so the men could fight overseas as soldiers, sailors etc.

The WAVES worked long hours. Many times, they would work Saturdays and Sundays without extra pay for their overtime.

"I was proud to be able to serve our country in any small thing I could do to fight off our enemy. From the Pacific coast we were mostly concerned with the Japanese."

JOHN R. HANEY

Branch of Service:
U.S. Marine Corps   (Corporal)
Years of Service:
January 1944 - August 1946   WWII
Outfit:
6th Marine Division
Areas Stationed:
California, Illinois, Arkansas, Guam
Ships:
U.S.S. Menifee (APA-202), U.S.S. Sanctuary
Specialty:
Ordinance Supply

On my Grandpa Haney's 17th birthday, he and his buddy, Ed, enlisted in the Marine Corps. They went to San Diego, California for eight weeks of boot camp, which my Grandpa remembers as being very tough and made men out of them real quick. He said it was an experience he would never want to relive, but at the same time, would not trade the experience.

Next, my Grandpa was chosen for Radio and Radar school. He attended two-months of training at the Manley School in Chicago, Illinois, then another two-months in Clarksville, Arkansas. He spent many long hours at school. They started early in the morning with only a quick break for dinner and then more school in the evening.

After completion of school, he went to San Francisco, California, where he worked in the Ordinance Supply Depot. At times it was difficult for him to travel from his boarding house to his job and back, because of all the blocked off roads and detours around the Cow Palace, where the formation of the United Nations was taking place. It was also during this time my Grandpa was shocked to learn that President Roosevelt had died. It was a very sad time and all the men were very somber.

My Grandpa (middle) with buddies at Camp Pendleton

The next stop was to Camp Pendleton, California, where he put in many hours of mess duty while awaiting orders to be shipped out.

Soon, he and his 6th Division boarded the U.S.S. Menifee, bound for Tsing Tao, China. Enroute, my Grandpa contracted jungle rot and was admitted to the naval hospital on Guam; the rest of the outfit went on to China. This was the time of the Hiroshima and Nagasaki atomic bombing and the Japs were about to surrender.

After almost six months in the Guam hospital, my Grandpa shipped back to California on the U.S.S. Sanctuary, and arrived home around Christmas time. He says the biggest thrill of his service time was sailing under the Golden Gate Bridge and knowing he was back in the good ol' U.S.A.

He then spent two-months in the naval hospital in San Leandro, California, before receiving his discharge in August of 1946. My Grandpa then went home to Deer Lake, Washington and married my Grandma.

My Grandma and Grandpa

FRANK JOHN HANNA

Branch of Service:
   U.S. Navy
Years of Service:
   September 1939 to August 1953   WWII
Outfit:
   Medical Detachment
Areas Stationed:
   Pacific
Ships:
   U.S.S. Helm DD-388 (Destroyer)
Specialty:
   Pharmacist Mate

   Mr. Hanna was the first of five brothers to enter the service. He enlisted at the age of 19-years old. He served with the Medical Detachment overseas for two years and earned two bronze stars, one was for his service in the Pearl Harbor engagement.

   The following is an article that appeared in the <u>Gila Bend, Arizona Newspaper</u>: Thursday, December 8, 1977.

Frank Hanna Witnessed Bombing of Harbor in WWII

   Pearl Harbor, Honolulu, Hawaii-December 7, 1941, thirty-six years ago to this date, Frank J. Hanna was there; Pharmacist Mate Third Class-USN. He was referred to as "Doc" aboard the U.S.S. Helm DD-388, a Destroyer.
   For several weeks prior to Pearl Harbor Day, Mr. Hanna

states that his ship had been on patrol duty, entering Pearl Harbor every 10 to 15-days for supplies and then back to patrol.

Hanna's own account:

"We had just entered the Harbor on Friday. Sunday morning at about 5:30 A.M., the Captain came aboard and had brought his 10-year-old son along. Our ship was to be moved from one end of the harbor to another area, and then the Captain and his son would leave for the day.

The ship got under way. We rounded 'Ford Island' and passed the seaplane ramps. The bow of our ship had just penetrated slightly the entrance to 'Westlock' (name of the mooring area for which we were headed).

I was sitting topside on the Fantail, contemplating going to Waikiki Beach as I had the day off. It was at this moment, that suddenly I heard some explosions, and looking toward Ford Island I saw several bombs hitting the seaplane ramps and buildings; hangers on the airfield were exploding and fire was shooting high into the air. I was stunned at first, and then, as the planes roared overhead, I could see the 'Rising Sun' emblem. Everyone aboard ship yelled, "The Japanese are bombing us!" Then, of course, the general quarters alarm was sounded.

The Captain 'backed' the ship up a few yards, and out the entrance of Pearl Harbor we proceeded. Pearl Harbor at that time had a very narrow channel; should a ship have been sunk in its mouth, the entrance would be impaired.

We were the first ship out of the harbor, and as we left this narrow channel there was a two-man Japanese submarine poised at the entrance. The Captain swerved the ship to avoid hitting it. A depth charge or two was dropped as we left the harbor for open water. We proceeded toward Waikiki Beach (there was a Coast Guard ship in that area) and the Captain transferred his son to the Coast Guard Ship.

During this time, a Japanese dive-bomber came after us. Fortunately, the bomb missed our side by several feet, but the explosion did rip part of the ship's bottom open; loosened some of the superstructure, radio equipment etc.

Wooden plugs, shoring and a pump kept the water out of the inside compartment that was damaged and heavy lines were used to secure the loosened super structure parts. Fortunately, no one was injured.

Within minutes of the first bomb attack, huge pillars of black smoke billowed from Pearl Harbor and you could see the sky full of planes; something like a swarm of bees.

We too had planes in the air at about the same time the Japanese attacked; we had an aircraft carrier 90-miles from Pearl Harbor and they had sent planes in to Pearl Harbor to land; normal procedure.

A fleet of B-17 Army Bombers was scheduled to land at Pearl Harbor from the U.S. We could see these B-17's, but at this moment, our planes were not geared for combat as such, though I understand some of them did happen to have some ammunition.

At first, no one could imagine what had gone wrong. In spite of the fact we had been on patrol for weeks prior to the attack. A Japanese Task Force was 'unaccounted for' by Naval Intelligence and Japanese Submarines had been sighted in many parts of the Pacific close to Pearl Harbor. Even during the attack, at least one two-man submarine was inside the harbor. (This submarine is a museum piece now.)

For the first time in months, practically all of the Pacific Fleet was in Pearl Harbor. It was a beautiful sight to see all our warships side by side in pairs and groups here and there in the harbor. Those battleships were considered impregnable fortresses. Three days later, when we re-entered Pearl Harbor, (for repairs) it was a ghastly sight.

Hawaii was a paradise prior to World War II. Beautiful Islands; only two hotels on Waikiki Beach at the time-the Royal Hawaiian and the Moana. One could see Diamond Head from all parts of the island.

Today, the scene has changed, as some of you know. Sometimes 'progress' destroys paradise, beauty and contentment."

December 1992

JAMES ALEXANDER HARDEN Jr. 1911 - 1986

Branch of Service:
  U.S. Navy
Years of Service:
  WWII - (30 years total service)
Areas Stationed:
  Pensacola, Florida; Saipan, Mariana Islands; Sitka,
  Alaska; Seattle, Washington; Astoria, Oregon
Ships:
  U.S.S. Constitution (and others)
Specialty:
  JAG and Pilot

Mr. Harden joined the Navy in 1930, and served on many ships. He was aid to the Island Commander of the Marianas. He was involved with the search for Amelia Earhart and went to his grave saying the plane was in the jungle when he was in Saipan.

After the war, he flew the mail route from Seattle, Washington to Sitka, Alaska for the government. His last duty station was Astoria, Oregon and was the pilot for the then Governor Snell of Oregon (1943 - 1947).

Mr. Harden worked his way up through the ranks and took every opportunity to take classes to advance his love for law and flying. However, he resented the fact that he did not have the opportunity to fly jets (due to age discrimination in 1960).

ALFRED D. HARRIS

Branch of Service:
   U.S. Army
Years of Service:
   4 years total service
   1968 - 1970 (Vietnam)
Outfit:
   1st Division, 2nd of the 28th Artillery Airborne
Areas Stationed:
   Ll Khe
Aircraft:
   Chinook Helicopter
Specialty:
   4.2 inch Artillery

Mr. Harris, along with five other men, were attached to a 4.2-inch mortar airborne unit. They were flown all over Vietnam to the hot spots where the troops were in need of help or mortar fire was needed. Mr. Harris was involved in the Tet Offensive in 1968, at Cho-Lon Air Base in Saigon.

The following is an article written by Chuck Dean (a friend of Mr. Harris and also a Vietnam Veteran)

What is a Vietnam Veteran?

Vietnam veterans are men and women. We are dead or alive, whole or maimed, sane or haunted. We grew from our experiences or we were destroyed by them or we struggle to find some place in between. We lived through hell or we had a pleasant, if scary adventure. We were Army, Navy,

Marines, Air Force, Red Cross, and civilians of all sorts. Some of us enlisted to fight for God and Country, and some were drafted. Some were gung-ho, and some went kicking and screaming.

Like veterans of all wars, we lived a tad bit (or a great bit) closer to death than most people like to think about. If Vietnam vets differ from others, perhaps it is primarily in the fact that many of us never saw the enemy or recognized him or her. We heard gunfire and mortar fire but rarely looked into enemy eyes. Those who did, like folks who encounter close combat anywhere and anytime, are often haunted for life by those eyes, those sounds, those electric fears that ran between ourselves, our enemies, and the likelihood of death for one of us. Or we get hard, calloused, tough. All in a day's work. But most of us remember and get twitchy, worried, sad.

We are crazies dressed in cammo, wide-eyed, wary, homeless and drunk. We are Brooks Brother's suit wearers, doing deals downtown. We are housewives, grandmothers, and church deacons. We are college professors engaged in the rational pursuit of the truth about the history or politics or culture of the Vietnam experience. And we are sleepless. Often sleepless.

We pushed paper; we pushed shovels. We drove jeeps, operated bulldozers, built bridges; we toted machine guns through dense brush, deep paddy, and thorn scrub. We lived on buffalo milk, fish heads and rice or C-rations. We did our time in high mountains drenched by endless monsoon rains or on the dry plains or on muddy rivers or at the most beautiful beaches in the world.

We wore berets, bandanas, flop hats and steel pots. Flak jackets, canvas, rash and rot. We ate cloroquine and got malaria anyway. We got shots constantly but have diseases nobody can diagnose. We spent our nights on cots or shivering in foxholes filled with waist-high water or lying still on cold wet ground, our eyes imagining Charlie behind every bamboo blade. Or we slept in hotel beds in Saigon or barracks in Thailand or in cramped ships' berths at sea.

We feared we would die or we feared we would kill. We simply feared, and often we still do. We hate the war or believe it was the best thing that ever happened to us. We blame Uncle Sam or Uncle Ho and their minions and secretaries and apologists for every wart or cough or tic of an eye. We wonder if Agent Orange got us.

Mostly--and this I believe with all my heart--mostly, we wish we had not been so alone. Some of us went with units; but many, probably most of us, were civilians one day, jerked up out of "the world," shaved, barked at, insulted, humiliated, de-egoized and taught to kill, to fix radios, to drive trucks. We went, put in our time, and were equally ungraciously plucked out of the morass and placed back in the real world. Our wives or husbands seemed distant and strange. Our friends wanted to know if we shot anybody.

And life went on, had been going on, as if we hadn't been there, as if Vietnam was a topic of political conversation or college protest or news copy, not a matter of life and death for tens of thousands.

Vietnam vets are people just like you. We served our country, proudly or reluctantly or ambivalently. What makes us different--what makes us Vietnam vets--is something we understand, but we are afraid nobody else will. But we appreciate your asking.

Vietnam veterans are white, black, beige and shades of gray; but in comparison with our numbers in the "real world," we were more likely black. Our ancestors came from Africa, from Europe, and China. Or they crossed the Bering

Sea Land Bridge in the last Ice Age and formed the nations
of American Indians, built pyramids in Mexico, or farmed
acres of corn on the banks of Chesapeake Bay. We had
names like Rodriguez and Stein and Smith and Kowalski.
We were Americans, Australians, Canadians, and Koreans;
most Vietnam veterans are Vietnamese.

We were farmers, students, mechanics, steelworkers,
nurses, and priests when the call came that changed us all
forever. We had dreams and plans, and they all had to
change...or wait. We were daughters and sons, lovers and
poets, beatniks and philosophers, convicts and lawyers. We
were rich and poor but mostly poor. We were educated or
not, mostly not. We grew up in slums, in shacks, in
duplexes, and bungalows and houseboats and hooches and
ranches. We were cowards and heroes. Sometimes we were
cowards one moment and heroes the next.

Many of us have never seen Vietnam. We waited at home
for those we loved. And for some of us, our worst fears were
realized. For others, our loved ones came back but would
never be the same.

We came home and marched in protest marches, sucked
in tear gas, and shrieked our anger and horror for all to hear.
Or we sat alone in small rooms, in VA hospital wards, in
places where only the crazy ever go. We are Republicans,
Democrats, Socialists, and Confucians and Buddhists and
Atheists--though as usually is the case, even the Atheists
among us sometimes prayed to get out of there alive.

We are hungry, and we are sated, full of life or clinging to
death. We are injured, and we are curers, despairing and
hopeful, loved or lost. We got too old too quickly, but some
of us have never grown up. We want, desperately, to go
back, to heal wounds, revisit the sites of our horror. Or we
want never to see that place again, to bury it, its memories,

its meaning. We want to forget, and we wish we could remember.

Despite our differences, we have so much in common. There are few of us who don't know how to cry, though we often do it alone when nobody will ask, "What's wrong?" We're afraid we might have to answer.

JOY M. HARRIS
(Joy "Connie" Caldaronello)

Branch of Service:
>   U.S. Army

Years of Service:
>   3 years

Outfit:
>   WAC 12th Army Group

Areas Stationed:
>   Georgia, France, and Germany

To be chosen as a WAC you must first have a reference of civilian background, technical abilities and physical and emotional stamina.

After being selected, special training for the women was held at Fort Oglethorpe, Georgia. There they were supplied with field equipment and were trained how to survive in the field of battle.

They were then sent to London, England and assigned to General Omar Bradley's 12th AGP Mobil Headquarters. They arrived to cold, wet weather and the beginning of the V-2 "Buzz" bomb attacks. This did not dampen their spirits and they looked forward to the challenges that lay ahead.

The first change that had to be made was from the dress uniform to the field uniform. This consisted of leggings, boots, trousers, combat jackets, and helmets.

Many lively discussions took place concerning the feasibility and safety of sending the women along with the 12th AGP FWD HQ, into France. The skeptics stated their fear of the women being captured and not being recognized as "protected personnel" under the rules of land and warfare. They would not be entitled to "Officer Prisoners" privileges. Others were concerned that the fighting efficiency of the men would be impaired by their worry over the WACS safety. Still others questioned whether the women could tolerate living in the rough field conditions.

On the other side of the argument, the officers declared that the WACS were very necessary and helpful to their offices. They stated the conditions in France would be no worse than that in London under the Buzz Bombs, which had not disrupted their work efficiency at all.

The WAC Staff Headquarters, after hearing both sides, viewed the WACS as necessary and capable, and it was decided to move them with their headquarters into France.

The WACS themselves were very eager to go. Many plans had to be made for clothing, maintenance, tents, etc. They participated in a very strenuous training and readiness program.

This first small selected contingent of WACS of the 12th Army Group Mobile Ground Forces, landed in Normandy on Omaha Beach, July 6, 1944. This was one month to the day after our fighting troops arrived. These women were clad in field uniforms, mastered the over side boat ladders, then motored ashore, and camped out in tents in an apple orchard. They did all their washing in helmets, slogged through mud and soldiered just like any other G.I.

Mrs. Harris and others from the 12th AG have put together a booklet of memories for the Women's War Memorial in Washington D.C. Historical manuscripts Collection (HMC) F#8-3.1

FRANCIS MARION HARRISON

Branch of Service:
    U.S. Army
Years of Service:
    WWII
Areas Stationed:
    US
Specialty:
    Medical Aid Man in Sub Dispensary

Mr. Harrison joined the Army at age 18. He received a commendation from Captain John B. Larson, U.S. Marine Corps, on December 27, 1944.

MICHAEL M. HAWKINS

Branch of Service:
    U.S. Army
Years of Service:
    19 years
    Deployed to Iraq for 1 year
Outfit:
    HHC 296 BsB, 2nd Infantry division, 3rd Stryker
    Brigade
Areas Stationed:
    Fort Lewis, Washington; Korea; Schofield Barracks,
    Hawaii; Fort Campbell, Kentucky; Germany
Aircraft:
    C5, C141, C130, Chinook, Blackhawk, Huey, Sherpa.
Specialty:
    Ammunition handling

"I have been many places, seen a lot of countries and met a lot of people. Being in the Army has taught me about people and their culture. The Army has also taught me about discipline, loyalty, freedom, and how to be a leader."

JAMES HOOVER

Branch of Service:
    U.S. Army
Years of Service:
    WWII (3 years and 3 months)
Outfit:
    Company A, 937th, Engineer Camouflage Battalion
Areas Stationed:
    United States, England, France, Belgium, Germany
Ships:
    Transported to England on the English Ship
    Mouratainia (February 1944)
Specialty:
    Camouflage Specialist

    Mr. Hoover served in an engineer camouflage Battalion that was attached to the Air Force. He spent many months training in the States before heading overseas.

    In England, he made dummy P-46 and P-47 fighter planes. They were painted exactly as the real planes. They were collapsed, packed in plywood boxes and sent to France. Possibly up to 500 of these planes were made.

    Mr. Hoover remembers one time he and his crew set up several of these dummy planes in a small wooded area. They were left there and he does not remember hearing of them drawing any enemy fire.

    In France, D+30, their camouflage work was mostly on gas tanks and fuel dumps. At that time the Germans were running low on fuel and were not making as many air attacks as earlier in the invasion. Therefore, his battalion was ordered to lay pierced plank parking stands and taxiways. Soon his battalion was split up and spread out to many different areas. Mr. Hoover's group joined the civilian contractors who were hired to repair the bombed out runways. His group helped them locate and obtain the supplies they needed.

Mr. Hoover has read many history accounts of the D-Day preparations, but has never read a word about the dummy airplanes. He has often wondered why some aspects of the invasion have been forgotten.

GLENN WALTER HUGHES

Branch of Service:
    U.S. Army (Sergeant)
Years of Service:
    March 1969 (drafted) - December 1971
    Total service time - 2 years, 9 months
Areas Stationed:
    "I was stationed at Safeguard Systems Command in
    Colorado Springs, Colorado. I was on detached service
    to Safeguard Systems Control at Red Stone Arsenal in
    Huntsville, Alabama. I was one of the very lucky ones."
Specialty:
    Communications

"I was one of the first Data Systems Terminal Equipment
Operators in the Army. I had a Top Secret-Crypto- RESDAT
(Restricted Data) CNWDI (Critical Nuclear Weapons Design
Information) security clearance. So my experiences were
interesting, exciting and classified. No big deal, just ancient
knowledge about ancient technology (now).

The worst part was coming home. The existing Veterans
groups really did not accept Vietnam era Veterans and the
newly established Vietnam Veterans group did not accept
those of us who had never been to Vietnam, so I was an
outcast. It was very difficult to get my life back after being
drafted."

DALE JACOBS

Branch of Service:
U.S. Navy
Years of Service:
1942 - 1945   WWII
Outfit:
APA-21
Ships:
U.S.S. Hornet and U.S.S. Crescent City
Specialty:
Mechanical Engineer (Machinist Mate Second Class)

Mr. Jacobs was drafted into the Army, but joined the Navy instead. He had 300 sheep to lamb before he could leave for service. The Navy gave him 3-months to get his affairs in order and then sent him to San Diego for 3-weeks of training. He then went to San Francisco and finally boarded a ship to Hawaii. There, he was transferred to the U.S.S. Hornet. He served in the mechanic department and worked as an engineer.

The Hornet was an aircraft carrier with an 803-foot straight runway flight deck. The Hornet had just returned from Japan after Doolittle's Tokyo Raid to pick up more aircraft.

October 26, 1942, the U.S.S. Hornet was sunk during the Battle of Santa-Cruz. Mr. Jacobs was in the forward engine room when the ship was hit by the Japanese bombs and torpedoes.

Aboard the ship were about 3,000 men, 300 of which were killed. Cruisers and destroyers that accompanied the fleet picked up the survivors and transported them to New

Caledonia. Tents were set up for the men until they could be re-assigned.

Mr. Jacobs was then assigned to the U.S.S. Crescent City APA-21 troop transport ship. They made four landings at Bougainville. During one landing, Mr. Jacobs had to beach and abandon the landing craft due to heavy gunfire. He returned the next day to recover it. He was later rewarded a medal for the recovery.

STAN JAFFE

Branch of Service:
    U.S. Army
Years of Service:
    July 1944 - November 1945
Areas Stationed:
    Texas, Philippines, Japan
Specialty:
    Infantry

Mr. Jaffe was in basic training at Camp Wolters, Texas from February 1944, to May 1944. He shipped out in August of 1944, and was at sea when the war ended and was slated as replacement for Americal Division for the Invasion of Japan. From the replacement depot, he was transferred to GHQ in Tokyo. He served in procurement and billeting until he returned to the states.

GLENN JAKUBOWSKI

Branch of Service:
   U.S. Army   (Cpl.)
Years of Service:
   1984 - 1988
Outfit:
   3rd Infantry Division
Areas Stationed:
   Germany and Texas
Specialty:
   Track Vehicle Mechanic and (unofficially) Weapons
   Expert

Mr. Jakubowski enjoyed the chance to travel and see places in the world that he would not have seen if it were not for the Army. He traveled all over Europe, to such places as Spain and Germany. He was in Europe during the Chernobyl Disaster. In Germany, he was attached to the Bravo Company, 1st & 15th Infantry. It was the same unit that Audie Murphy was in.

During the REFORGER (Return of Forces to Germany) Mr. Jakubowski was in Grafenwier, Germany. He maintained the track vehicles and was able to drive the Bradleys and fire their weapons systems.

Mr. Jakubowski was accepted to fly the Apache Helicopter just before health issues caused him a premature retirement from the military.

Mr. Jakubowski was an extra in the movie "For the Boys" starring James Caan and Bette Middler. He was in the Vietnam scene.

WILLIAM A. JAMES

Branch of Service:
>U.S. Army   (E-4)

Years of Service:
>Vietnam; 2 years, 6 months, 14 days

Outfit:
>1st Aviation Brigade, 271st (13 months)
>147th ASHC (Assault Support Helicopter Company)
>>(5 months)

Areas Stationed:
>Fort Lewis, Washington - A.I.T. (Advanced Individual
>>Training) - (4 months)

Aircraft:
>CH-47; Chinook Helicopter

Specialty:
>Helicopter Repairman/Flight Crew - "Innkeeper 003"

"I was sent to Vietnam in 1970, and spent 18-months there. During the first 13-months, I was part of a 5-man crew on a Chinook Helicopter (CH-47A). I started out as a door gunner, then a Crew Chief, then became a Flight Engineer. My rank was E-4 (Specialist 4th Class). At this point, I could tell the pilots to take us home (with good reason) and they would be in trouble if they did not.

My ship could pick up 12 tons on the cargo hook and could hold 8 tons inside. We could get a jeep, a 3/4 ton (like a pickup without its top) and a small trailer inside. The most Vietnam soldiers I ever carried totaled 96, plus our crew. It was pretty crowded in there with that many little people, and let me tell you, they really smelled bad.

Most of our trips were re-supply or troop movements.

Although, one unusual load was to carry a water buffalo. The net we used was probably 16-feet square with big 'D' rings on each corner. The owners of the water buffalo convinced it to walk onto the net. When we lifted off the ground, the net pulled tight like a marble bag. The holes of the net were large enough so its legs dangled through the holes. Away we went. I wish I knew if it was scared or not.

I quit flying when I went into the 147th. They had to 'wax' their helicopters and I thought they were already a big enough target."

JAMES F. JOHNSON

Branch of Service:
   U.S. Navy   (Commander)
Years of Service:
   Active Duty: June 1961 - September 1969
   Naval Reserve Duty: 12 years - (20 years total)
Outfits:
   VS-28, VP-2
Areas Stationed:
   Quonset Point, Rhode Island; Whidbey Island,
   Washington; Iwakuni, Japan; Pensacola, Florida
Ships:
   U.S.S. Wasp
Specialty:
   Intelligence Officer
   Naval Flight Officer (Navigator and Tactical
      Coordinator)
   Instructor at the Naval Aviation Officer Candidate
      School

1/62 - 1/63: VS-28, Quonset Point, Rhode Island:

"I was the intelligence officer in this anti-submarine
squadron. Our home base was Naval Air Station, Quonset
Point, Rhode Island. We deployed aboard the carrier U.S.S.
Wasp (CVS-18). I was an Ensign during my 12-months with
VS-28. After being commissioned out of the Navy's Aviation
Officer Candidate School in October 1961, I attended an
Intelligence Officer school at Norfolk NAS, and upon
graduation was assigned to VS-28. As the squadron
Intelligence Officer, I briefed all flights. The highlight of my

service with VS-28 was participating in the 'Cuban Missile Crisis' in October 1962. The Wasp was in Cuban waters locating and inspecting outgoing Soviet vessels, which carried missiles out of Cuba. My job was briefing hops every 4-hours around the clock for several days.

Being around aviators for a year, I got the urge to fly. I applied for Navigation Training and was accepted. From February to December 1963, I was in the Training Command and earned my Wings as a Naval Flight Officer. I was assigned to VP-2."

12/63 - 9/66: VP-2, Whidbey Island, Washington:

"I was a member of a flight crew (as Navigator and Tactical Coordinator) whose mission was anti-submarine warfare. My 'ground job' was the squadron's Intelligence Officer. While with VP-2, we deployed to the Aleutian Islands and Japan. In the Aleutian Islands, we flew patrols out of Kodiak, Adak and Shemya to the far reaches of the Pacific.

We deployed to Marine Corps Air Station, Iwakuni, Japan in 1965 and 1966. While in Japan, we received orders to detach four aircraft (we had twelve in the squadron) to Saigon, Vietnam. We did so and flew patrols from the 17th parallel south around the southern tip of Vietnam and up the west coast to the Cambodian border. We were looking for boats bringing supplies into South Vietnam."

9/66 - 9/69: Naval Aviation Officer Candidate School, Naval Air Station, Pensacola, Florida:

"I served my last 3-years of active duty as an Instructor in the Naval Aviation Officer Candidate School.

After active duty, I served in the Naval Reserve until I had 20-years of service. I retired with the rank of Commander (O-5, equal to a LT. Colonel in the Army).

Please understand that I am no hero, which I state with no false modesty. The real heroes are those who endured years of imprisonment and abuse by the North Vietnamese and those who rest in various military cemeteries around the world."

WALTER A. JOHNSON

Branch of Service:
    U.S. Navy
Years of Service:
    1969 - 1973 (Honorable Discharge - 1973)
    Republic of South Vietnam: 1970 - 1971 & 1972 - 1973
    Naval Reserve: 1973 - 1975
Areas Stationed:
    San Diego, California (boot camp and service school)
        1969 - 1970
    USNAVSUPPACT Danang, RVN 1970 - 1971
    NAVSTA Kodiak, Alaska 1971 - 1972
    U.S.S. Midway (CVA-41) 1972 - 1973
Ships:
    U.S.S. Midway (CVA-41)
Specialty:
    Commissary Man, Petty Officer 3rd Class

"It was an honor to serve in the world's greatest NAVY. My thanks to all those who served before me, and to those who serve now, and to all those who will serve in the future. My peace and prayers for their safety."

EDGAR W. JONES

Branch of Service:
    U.S. Navy
Years of Service:
    October 1942 - February 1946 WWII
Outfit:
    Cub 7, Special NCB 17 and attached to a Marine
        Division
Areas Stationed:
    South Pacific (from New Guinea to Philippines)
Specialty:
    Hospital Corpsman - Phm 1/c

"I went into the Navy at age 15, and trained in the medical field. I served at Mare Island in California, and went overseas in November of 1943. I served for 27-months in the South Pacific on many different islands and bases.
    I am a disabled veteran and received compensation."

Mr. Jones earned two battle stars during his service.

LLOYD KEELAND

Branch of Service:
　U.S. Marine Corps
Years of Service:
　1943 - 1946　WWII
Outfit:
　I Company, 3rd Battalion, 23rd Regiment, 4th Division
Areas Stationed:
　San Diego, California (Boot Camp); Camp Pendleton, California (Infantry Training); Maui, Hawaii; Iwo Jima; Guam; San Francisco, California (Discharge)
Ships:
　Troop Transports, LSTs
　U.S.S. Bon Homme Richard (aircraft carrier)
Specialty:
　Machine Gun Squad (Iwo Jima)
　Truck Driver (Guam)

The following is an excerpt from the book --
   The Lusty Life of Loon Lake Lloyd:
   WWII Marine, Logger and Resort Owner
   by Lloyd and Ellen Keeland

IWO JIMA

We'd been on board ship a long time by the time we had
sailed from Hawaii to Iwo Jima, an island seven hundred
miles south of Japan. The day was just breaking when our
huge convoy of hundreds of ships arrived.

For days, B-29 airplanes had been dropping bombs, and
battleships and destroyers had bombarded the five-mile long
volcanic island with sixteen-inch guns trying to hit Japanese
pillboxes, bunkers and strongholds for the initial landing.

It didn't do much good because all the 22,000 Japanese
were securely dug in down in the bowels of the earth. They
had dug twenty-six miles of tunnels and converted the old
sulphur mines and natural caves into living quarters. For
ten months, General Kuribayashi worked his men around
the clock, sometimes all but four hours a day to fortify the
airstrips and island. The small Japanese village had been
evacuated and buildings dismantled. With the help of
hundreds of captured Korean laborers, an oak forest on the
island was felled and used to shore up the tunnels. Cement
entranceways and ceilings were poured from six inches to
ten feet thick. All entrances were angled at ninety degrees a
few feet inside for protection against flame-throwers,
artillery and demolition charges. Some tunnels were a
hundred feet below ground, with huge hundred by forty foot
rooms. Bunks were carved into the sides and all the walls
were plastered. Steam, electricity and water were piped in.
The water was from a well and a seawater distilling plant.

166

Air vents were cleverly put in everywhere and so were the holes from which they fired rifles, machine guns, mortars, artillery, and rocket launchers. They even had tanks buried with just their big guns sticking out.

There I was in the third landing wave. I had a backpack on my back, a gas mask hanging around my neck, an M-1 rifle, and a cartridge belt around my waist, from which hung a bayonet and a canteen.

Over the ship's edge, we went down a cargo net. We climbed down that to a landing craft that's a-bouncing up and down. You try to time it just right to turn loose of the net and you're in. The sea was rough.

We looked out on our way in and saw landing craft being blown up, bodies and metal flying everywhere, the sea turning red. Rifle shells were hitting the side of the craft and we stayed hunkered down there waiting for the Higgins boat to hit the beach. There she hit. When the ramp went down if you're on the right you're supposed to head towards the right a little bit, and if you're on the left you run out there to the left, and if you're in the center you work out there straight ahead. But all you did is run out to a bunch of people piled up there on the beach. So much crossfire no way anyone could move. Shells, bullets, shrapnel, everything flying; so much metal in the air I don't know how anyone survived.

Our squad, packing machine guns, tripods and ammo boxes, was moving right along zigzagging up the steep, soft sand dune, looking for a break in the heavy firing to get through. I got hit with shrapnel in the knee, and the corpsman who was running right with us told me to go back to the ship. I hobbled back past a lot of men lying on the beach begging me to take them with me. We had been instructed to let the stretcher bearers carry off the wounded

167

so I boarded a Higgins boat full of wounded and returned to the ship. There a ship's corpsman stapled up my knee and bandaged it and I went and sat on the deck. There all around me were men blown to hell moaning and hollering. Some had no arms, no legs, and I thought who wants to sit and listen to that? Not me! I caught another landing craft to the beach. Only this time the Navy coxswain must have been a new guy. He was one scared boy. The first thing he did was go under the bow of the ship. That was his first boo-boo. "Big Mo," the big sixteen-inch gun aboard ship was touched off, deafening all of us in the boat below. That boom impaired the hearing in my right ear the rest of my life; I never could hear anything out of it very much. I imagine the rest of those guys were the same way. We got turned around and we were getting in pretty close to the beach when a mortar shell hit right in front of us. The Navy ensign stopped the boat. The Marine lieutenant jumped up and put a .45 pistol to the kid's head and said, "You'll go forward and put these men ashore."

I imagine the Navy kid was even scareder when the .45 was against his head so we went forward and pretty soon, we were scraping sand. The ramp flopped down and the Marines never hesitated, but leapt out full force. Then the kid must have gotten excited again because all of a sudden the ramp closed again, piling men down on top of one another as they were trying to get out. Some were hanging on the top of it, some were half-way over, when the kid must have realized his mistake and opened the ramp again. I was still in the boat but got off with the rest of them this time. My outfit wasn't hard to find, they hadn't went much, over close to the airstrip.

We were a machine gun outfit and here's how we ran along. The head gunner, the guy running the machine gun, he packed the gun and one belt of ammunition. The assistant gunner carried the tripod and the ammunition carrier. I was an assistant gunner. It wasn't but a few days that I was a head gunner, replacing the other gunners killed and wounded.

After a few days of hard fighting, we took the airstrip and those other jokers raised the flag.

We had numbers stenciled on our back, which represented where we were from. On our dungaree shirt jackets was something that looked like this:

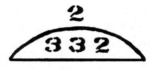

The half a circle shape signified the Fourth Marine Division. The first "three" meant the Twenty-Third Regiment, the second "three" was for the Third Battalion, the "two" inside the shape was for I Company, and the "two" on top was for my rank as a corporal. This stenciled emblem was right in the middle of the back, made a good target. The coded numbers were to throw the Japs off in case they a got hold of us. We were supposed to tell them nothing, only our name and our rank. The numbers were also to identify us on the battlefield. We removed all our other rank and unit insignias and left them in Maui.

The black sulphur-smelling sand was so hard to get around in that the tanks and Cats and other equipment on the beach had a hard time moving inland. They put down woven steel mats of different sizes, some fifty by a hundred foot long. You could see those mats flipping through the air like playing cards, so many bombs were hitting.

Sneaking around all these Japs in their hidey holes you knew they were close when you could hear "Clap, clap!" the sound of the Jap soldiers breaking open their hand grenades on their helmets. Then they'd drop back in their tunnels. The bombs never stopped. Oh no, Ol' "Washing Machine Charlie" just kept them dropping all night long, day and night, steady as a washing machine. I took some shrapnel in my arm, which is still there. Some of the shrapnel in my knee worked out years later.

Oh, this Walt Berry, he had a machine gun platoon. And we had a machine gun platoon. The lieutenant brought an Italian cook up there and put him in Berry's squad. Most of our whole company was Italian, out of New York and New Jersey. Berry was always in awful rough places. This time he was up on a rock cliff. We had our machine gun set up right below him. He was next to us, up high. They passed the word down for everybody to hold fire. Never did know what that was all about. Sergeant Ayers was in the foxhole right next to us. He stood up and that crazy ding-a-ling replacement cook cut him right in half with a machine gun. He killed one fine guy. I liked that guy. The cook was screaming and bawling-he was making more noise than the Japs were. It didn't take the corpsmen long to come and get that cook out of there. They gave him some kind of shot and got a stretcher and packed him out. Then they packed Ayers out.

The Japanese were banzaiing. That night from our foxholes, we had heard a big group of Japs below us drinking their Sake and getting primed for the attack. It just sounded like they were going nuts, chanting and yelling. We were up

above in rocks and crags, and they were down below. They
weren't sure where we were and we had orders to stay quiet.
We let them get coming good, howling and screaming and
then shot a parachute flair along with a mortar, which lit
things up real good, just like daylight. We didn't need orders
to start firing. When that ol' flair went up and popped, that's
when it all broke loose.

Walt Berry and I threw hand grenades during that banzai
attack until our arms got sore. The Japanese couldn't tell
where hand grenades were coming from. When you fire that
.30 caliber machine gun, they know right where you're at.
This is because every fifth round, or bullet, is a tracer, just a
ball of fire so you can see where it goes; you can see what
you're hitting. We picked them off just like shooting ducks,
but they kept right on a-coming. We mowed them down
right and left. None of the banzaiing Japs got through to us,
none of them in that bunch.

Boy, we had a pile of those slant-eyed son-of-a-guns out
there the next morning. That's where we ran into those
Imperial Guard Marines. Yes, Japs had big, tall Marines
wrapped in cheesecloth. A bullet would go right through
them and they'd keep on coming.

We were in the same place five or six days. We finally
moved forward and looked around for a place to dig in for
the night. The guys were starting to shovel. In lots of places,
the sand was too hot to lay down on, kind of a black, ground
up volcanic rock. About that time, we saw huge metal doors
open and a framework came up on railroad tracks out of the
ground. An explosive charge was set with a deafening
"BOOM!" releasing a huge garbage can-shaped projectile.
We had been hearing this screaming "Tokyo Express" bomb,
as we called it, but never knew where it was coming from.
The noise it made was like an air-borne locomotive "wo-op,

wo-op, wo-op," lobbing end over end in every direction. It screamed like nothing you've ever heard before and it would scare you because you didn't know where it was going to go. It never did any damage but sailed clear over the island, landing in the ocean. We radioed in its position and next morning the Marine Corsair planes dropped napalm on it; enough that the demolitions men could run in there and throw satchel charges of TNT dynamite in the hole. The enemy wouldn't be using that one for a while, until they dug the boulders and dirt out of it.

In the Marine Corps we had been issued a solid brass emblem-you know it's the world with an anchor and an eagle-this one was about an inch and a half across-a little heavy thing. One guy had been shot and fallen on his face. The corpsman came to pick him up and I was there and helped. We took off his backpack and his clothes; we were trying to find out where he'd been hit. We couldn't find any wound or blood anywhere; we looked everywhere. We even looked in his hair. Then we noticed that Jap bullet had hit him square in the back and stuck right there in that brass emblem. He was carrying the Marine Corps emblem in his backpack. The concussion had just knocked the wind out of him. That Marine Corps emblem had saved his life. His name was PFC Neal Markley. He had a trucking business in Oakdale, California. Fifty-five years later, I found him through the Fourth Marine Division Association, and we have talked over the phone.

Anyway, he was there in that mixup; we had advanced right up to this...like a big bluff in front of us. That's where we got pinned down in a hole about the size of a living room. As we were deciding where to set up the machine guns, Tim Shay and I were standing there talking to one another, and he says, "You got hit there, too?"

I was limping, and I says, "No, that was opening day." As we talked, "Boom," he dropped to the ground. A sniper's bullet hit him right between the eyes. I called for a corpsman and he was hit dead center. Packed him out of there. That was a shame, that was one fine fellow. I dug in right there, and tried to draw fire. It was the front line. Some of the other guys saw the yellow smoke from that sniper; they tore right after him. We had overrun that sniper. He was in the back of us. He was up on a twenty-foot-high hill a bulldozer had made. Frank Kallinger shot him. The shot tumbled him right out of there.

"Ha, ha, ha. Got him," Frank said.

We were there a long time from morning to must have been evening when they made a big smoke screen and we were able to get out of there. With the smoke screen, the Japs couldn't see anything. I think the artillery laid 'em back in there, too, kept them in their holes long enough for us to get out. The stretcher-bearers were able to come in and get PFC Markley out.

We had the machine guns set up, but there was nothing to shoot at; we were picking them off with the rifles. Then that one Jap committed Hari Kari. He must have been hit or thought he'd get it anyway. He looked up toward the sun, took that knife and stuck it right in the middle of his belly and that was the end of him, he tumbled off of the bank.

One night Frank Kallinger and I were in a big bomb hole-which made a good foxhole-there were plenty of them around, tailor-made. A Jap might be in one next to you, though, so you'd better look around.

We weren't supposed to fire that night in a no-fire restriction. I had done my watch and I woke Frank up. It was his turn, so he was on watch and I went to sleep. A little

later, I woke up with the clanging of a sword hitting a rifle
barrel, "Clack, clack, clack, clack!" Frank must have dozed
off because a Japanese man was at the edge of our bomb
crater trying to hit him with a three-foot long Samurai
sword.

Frank was fending him off with his rifle barrel. His hand
was cut. He must have grabbed the sword because all his
tendons were cut on his right hand. I finally got awake
enough to see what was going on, it don't take you very long,
either. I got the Jap by the ankles and jerked him down in
the shell hole with us, then had to do him in the best way we
could do 'er. We used the entrenching shovel to finish him
off. Couldn't shoot, no firing that night. Frank had a hand
he had the rest of his life-it stayed curled up, he couldn't
even get his fingers all the way open. Bea, his wife, called
them his "bird claws" when she'd get made at him. Lucky he
had any fingers.

I passed the word to the guy next to us in his shell hole
thirty feet away, "Need a corpsman." The word was passed
down the line.

Then the word was passed back, "A corpsman's coming,"
so you wouldn't shoot him. Well, you couldn't shoot...we
were expecting a banzai attack; we wanted to surprise them.
So, I guess, the idea was to wait until they made their big
charge, and then dump it on them. But no charge happened,
the enemy stayed put.

We weren't supposed to take any souvenirs home, but I
brought that Samurai sword back with me after the war.

One time we dug in; that was about all the time. They
passed up, along the line, some rations. One guy, Hartman,
from Oklahoma, was complaining about the rations.

I said, "Well, if you don't like that, cut a steak off of one of
those burning blank-blank's there."

174

Those burning Japs were lying all over the place. He left us and went 'way out by himself in his own little hole.

We thought we were lucky to get anything to eat.

Then there was King, who was a replacement from the field music outfit. He must have been straight off the ship because he sat around there and kept saying, "Oh, if Daddy could only see me now. If Daddy could only see me now."

We were on the move and we stopped in one of those gosh-darned shell craters and them Japs were up above us. We were pinned down again, which was nothing new. We were in the low ground; they were in the high ground. So we had the machine gun set up there watching for when they'd fire; there'd be a little yellow smoke or something-we'd machine gun that. This Japanese joker came up out of a hole, a hundred feet right in front of us; we didn't even know there was a cave there.

I threw the rifle up to my shoulder and King knocked it down saying, "Hey, don't shoot, he's a human being!"

Boy, it's a lucky thing somebody else bore sighted him 'cause he was loaded to blow us all up. I don't know what happened to King, he disappeared, too. They probably got him to packing out dead or back on the beach in supplies. I doubt his Daddy would have been very proud of him to pull a stunt like that.

The Japs had the Nambu machine gun. We were using ones out of WWI. Shoot, all ours would put out is about 550 rounds a minute. The Japs were putting out about a thousand rounds a minute. We had the light machine gun, a .30 caliber. The heavy one was water-cooled, but we converted it and used it on a light machine gun tripod-that way we didn't pack that infernal water tank around with us.

Why did they do away with that old faithful M-1? Oh,

they "needed more fire-power, needed more fire-power!"
You could drag that rifle through sand, mud, dirt, whatever,
and that ol' baby would still fire. I never did see one of them
jam. Never. If it did, it was faulty ammunition. I hated to
turn mine in. They took our M-1's and issued us .30 caliber
carbines and .45 pistols, although some rifle platoons were
able to keep their M-1's. The .30 caliber carbine was short,
only made for jungle fighting. It would shoot just a little
further than the .45 pistol. Neither shot as far as the M-1.
One well-placed shot is all that is needed and that's exactly
what the M-1 could deliver. They don't need to tell us that
was a new type of jungle warfare. More political thinking-
someone paid someone off and told Uncle Sam they needed
a new weapon. That M-1 was an accurate, faithful and long-
shooting rifle. It had them all beat. The Japs had three
different caliber of rifles-a .31, a 6.65 and 7.7, all good
weapons.

Many years later, Frank Kallinger, the Marine who had
the tendons of his hand cut by grabbing the Samurai sword,
found out where I lived through one of my customers. The
man used to come up here to get this real fancy maple and
myrtle. He used it in making furniture. I got to visiting with
him one evening and we got to fighting the war again and I
told him about Frank. I hadn't seen him since the corpsman
took him away. I think he got hit again, down on the beach,
waiting to be evacuated, because he had a big scar on his
shoulder and shrapnel all in his chest. I told this guy when
Frank joined the service he lived in Whittier and wrote to his
wife there.

He said, "If he's still in California, I'll find him!"

Boy, about a week, ten days, the ol' phone was a-ringing-
in those days all we had was the old radio phone. It was
Frank.

176

"Boy, I'm coming up there!" And boy, he was here. He had a month or two to go to retire from U.S. Steel and he bought a house on Hinder Road in Elkton before he left here from that first visit. He moved up and together we had many a happy hunting and fishing trip. One year he developed pneumonia and passed away. The Sergeant Major upstairs called him to his final reward.

Another morning we had been dug in all night. It was almost daylight when we saw four Japs hotfooting along a trail there-all of a sudden they stopped.

"Ah, they went into a hole," I said, seeing them go into a shell crater where a bomb had dropped. They had come out of some caves nearby and went into that hole in the ground.

We passed the word down the line, "Don't shoot." We took some .30 caliber rifles and machine guns and snuck up to the edge of the hole. They were dug in there chattering away. I don't know what they were saying, but it must have been something to the effect that-what they thought they'd do is wait 'til about daylight and pick a few of us off. We weren't close enough to the edge yet to see them, but we could hear them. Three of us circled it and started lobbing hand grenades in it. Then we ran up there and finished them off; they were hurt. We got trouble for that by that goofy lieutenant who we had only for a day with the rifle platoon. I think what made him mad was that we were banzaiing the Japs. But we never saw him anymore, he left the rifle platoon. Us machine gunners never did have any lieutenant. They wouldn't stay with us at all. All our outfit was so rough we couldn't keep an officer; they'd go over to mortars-transfer out of machine guns. So we just ran on Iwo without one. Actually, by the eighteenth of March, the end of the battle, there wasn't much of I Company left. Out of the 250 men that landed, there was only thirteen men of the company left. It was about the same with all the companies. After twenty-eight days of battle, there were 6,000 American men killed, and 20,000 wounded. The Japs sustained 21,000 killed, and one thousand were taken prisoner; so few because most of them, when cornered or trapped, would commit Hari Kari rather than surrender. I was one of the few men who could say they landed on D-Day and made it all the way through the battle of Iwo Jima.

PHILIP DAVID KIPPEN

Branch of Service:
    U.S. Navy
Years of Service:
    1992 - 1996 (end of first Iraq conflict)
Outfit:
    U.S.S. Lake Erie (Pre-commission)
    NCTAMS EastPac (Naval Telecommunications
        Command)
Areas Stationed:
    Pearl Harbor, Hawaii
Ships:
    U.S.S. Lake Erie
Specialty:
    Radioman

"From Boot Camp, I went to a pre-commission unit for the U.S.S. Lake Erie where we finished up the building process on the Lake Erie. We set sail to Pearl Harbor, Hawaii on her maiden voyage taking her through the Panama Canal and commissioning her in July of 1993.

After a two-year tour on the Lake Erie, I took a new assignment at NCTAMS EastPac in Hawaii. There I worked on building an intelligence profiling system for the Joint Intelligence Command-Pacific Fleet. I stayed there until the end of my enlistment in 1996.

I had a great deal of fun during my enlistment and learned quite a bit in the process. Enlisting in the Navy was one of the best things I did in my life. It taught me respect, responsibility and honor. I don't ever regret the time I spent in the service."

KENNETH W. KREITZ

Branch of Service:
  U.S. Marine Corps   (Corporal)
Years of Service:
  WWII and Korea
Outfit:
  1st Marine Division, 3rd Armored Amphibian (Track-Vehicle) AMTRAC
Areas Stationed:
  San Francisco, California; Okinawa; Korea
Specialty:
  Rifleman - Track Driver

Mr. Kreitz and his outfit were involved in the Battle for Okinawa and the Invasion of Peleliu.

The Third Provisional Armored Amphibian Battalion received a citation for their involvement in the Invasion of Peleliu, September of 1944. They not only fought courageously against the well-hidden and fortified Japanese, but also fought in temperatures of 120-degrees with only small amounts of drinking water available. Finally, after hard fighting, they secured the strategic air and land base for the future operations in the Pacific.

They also received a citation for extraordinary heroism in action during the Battle of Okinawa, April to June 1945. They waged a fierce battle with the Japanese to secure the enemy bastion at Shuri Castle. Then they fought across heavily fortified ridges to trap the enemy on the Oroku Peninsula.

In 1951, Mr. Kreitz was in Korea and again his First Marine Division received a citation. This time for destroying and routing enemy forces north of the Hwachon Reservoir. The Division reduced the enemy's main fortified complex, which was on the 38th parallel. They advanced the front against enemy forces in the "Punch Bowl" area, which completed the liberation of South Korea in that area.

Mr. Kreitz earned many awards for his service in the U.S. Marine Corps. He was awarded Presidential Unit Citation Ribbons and Bronze Stars for his service on Peleliu, Okinawa, and Korea; The Asiatic-Pacific Campaign Medal; Victory Medal for World War II; National Defense Service Medal; Korean Service Medal; and the United Nations Service Medal.

RICHARD LACZAVICS

Branch of Service:
   U.S. Marine Corps
Years of Service:
   Korea, 8 years
Outfit:
   1st Marine Division
Areas Stationed:
   Quantico, VA; Camp Pendleton, CA; Korea
Ships:
   MST-5 Phoenix; U.S.S. Talladega; U.S.S. Nelson Walker
Specialty:
   Machine Gunner - Small Arms Mechanic

One of the experiences Mr. Laczavics remembers during his time at Quantico was when he was working as a M.P. at the main gate and had to call to an officer driving a car to stop. The officer did not stop, so Mr. Laczavics was required to shoot into the cars trunk. The officer stopped!

Mr. Laczavics shipped to Korea at the age of 16-years old. He was involved in the Inchon Landing, where he saw many of his friends lose their lives in the fighting. Many of these memories still haunt him to this day.

His job at Camp Matthews in Korea was as a rifle range coach. He came home in 1953.

RUTH LACZAVICS

Branch of Service:
   U.S. Air Force
Years of Service:
   1950 - 1953
Outfit:
   Communications and Special Services
Areas Stationed:
   McCord A.F.B. Tacoma, Washington
Specialty:
   Teletype Maintenance

   "There were so many amusing experiences during my military career. I transferred to special services (I was the only woman there) so I could teach ceramics at the base hobby shop. I made friends with all the A.P.'s and the officers. When I did something stupid, they all knew it was me, but no one ratted on me. It pays to have friends in high places!"

HOWARD LAUTER

Branch of Service:
> U.S. Army

Years of Service:
> 3 years   WWII

Outfit:
> Company "H", 164th Infantry Division
> (Americal Division)

Areas Stationed:
> Guadalcanal, Suva, Fiji, Bougainville, Philippines

Specialty:
> Heavy Mortars - Rifleman

Mr. Lauter and his Division provided support for the 1st Marine Division during the Battle for Henderson Field on Guadalcanal. The heavy fighting started August 6, 1942, and lasted until the island was finally secured on February 9, 1943.

Many men were killed during the heavy fighting. Mr. Lauter remembered talking to his Sergeant one moment and then, as he turned to leave him, a Japanese sniper shot and killed him. Mr. Lauter always wondered why the Jap chose the Sergeant rather than himself.

In addition to the fierce fighting, the soldiers had to endure many adverse conditions. Much of the time, the high temperatures and the monsoon rains would make life miserable. They also had to beware of the possibility of coral poisoning, malnutrition, and malaria, due to the many types of vile insects and rodents found on the island.

ALICE ADAMS LAVIS

Branch of Service:
    U.S. Marine Corps Women's Reserve
Years of Service:
    WWII: Active Duty, March 1944 - March 1946
    Inactive Reserve until March 1950
Areas Stationed:
    Boot Camp; Camp Lejeune, North Carolina
        (May - June 1944)
    Headquarters Marine Corps; Arlington, Virginia
        Henderson Hall (June 1944 - April 1945)
    Officer Training; Camp Lejeune, North Carolina
        (April - July 1945)
    Marine Corps Base; San Diego, California
        (August 1945 - March 1946)
Specialty:
    HQMC - secretarial support (PFC and Corporal)
    San Diego - Mess Officer (Second Lieutenant)

"Women were recruited into the Marine Corps beginning in February 1943, under the slogan, 'Free a Marine to Fight.' We held many jobs such as aircraft maintenance, truck driving, supply corps, and all clerical chores. We were called 'Women Marines' or 'WRs' and did not have a nickname or acronym, as did the WACS, WAVES, and SPARS (Coast Guard Women).

One of the most memorable experiences I had happened in April 1945, when I was a Corporal. I was one of the approximately 200 women Marines stationed in Washington D.C. who marched in the funeral procession for President Franklin D. Roosevelt.

The experiences of living and working with young women from all over the country, and being part of the United States Marine Corps, were invaluable and I have never forgotten them. As they say, 'Once a Marine, Always a Marine!' "

FREDDY LEGARE

Branch of Service:
    U.S. Army   (Sergeant T-4)
Years of Service:
    March 1943 - October 1945
Outfit:
    Tank Destroyer - 635th CO. C
Areas Stationed:
    England, France, Germany, Holland, Belgium
Specialty: Machine Gunner and Cook

Mr. Legare was a Technical Sergeant during WWII. He volunteered to enter the service because he knew that if he did not he would be drafted. He was inducted into the U.S. Army at Fort Lewis, Washington. There he was issued his uniforms and full equipment. After only five or six days, he was sent to Camp Hood, Texas for war service training and preparations.

Mr. Legare was assigned to a detached outfit and sent to Europe. The outfit was placed in any area that weak points could be found on the front lines. His Company never knew from day to day what they would be involved in.

Mr. Legare fought in the Battle of the Bulge. In his 'C' Company, three men were lost total.

During the Invasion of Normandy, June 9, 1944, Mr. Legare was on the beach. His birthday is on June 10, so he spent his 27th birthday in a foxhole. He survived the Invasion where many had lost their lives for their country.

PIERRE LIEURANCE

Branch of Service:
    U.S. Navy
Years of Service:
    1942 - 1946 WWII
Aircraft:
    Corsair, AT-6, Stearman
Specialty:
    Taxied aircraft to areas where they were needed and
    Flight Instructor

    My Uncle Pierre served in the Navy during WWII. He had the opportunity to work around many of the different warplanes. Depending on where a plane was needed, he would move the aircraft from field to field. He was also a Flight Instructor, but found that most of the newer pilots already had the training they needed before they arrived in his class. He remembers having a lot of down time because of this and his classes got smaller and smaller as the war came to a close.

JACK LIPPUS

Branch of Service:
>   Was on contract to U.S. War Department by the
>   Bendix Corporation.

Years of Service:
>   1940 - 1967

Outfit:
>   All Military Units

Areas Stationed:
>   All U.S. States

Aircraft:
>   P-38, P-40, P-51, B-17, B-24, B-25, B-26, F-100, F-102,
>   F-104, KC-130

Specialty:
>   Aircraft Engines

Mr. Lippus' job was to look for problems with certain aircraft engines. He worked on the B-25's that participated in the "Doolittle's Raid." He also worked on many other different aircraft and met many famous people such as Jimmy Doolittle, Howard Hughes, and many famous aces.

One time Mr. Lippus had the opportunity to sit in the Spruce Goose while the engines were running. If Mr. Hughes decided for some reason one of the engines did not operate well because of carburetor problems, they would remove it and take it to the Bendix shop (which manufactured the carburetors) and put it on their test bench.

Nicholas Rider and Jack Lippus, March 2004

MARCOS MADRIGAL

Branch of Service:
   U.S. Marine Corps
Years of Service:
   Vietnam
Outfit:
   1st Marine Corps, 5th Marine
Areas Stationed:
   MCRD San Diego, California (training)
   Camp Pendleton, California
   Vietnam (30 miles south of DaNang)

Marcos Madrigal (left) with a buddy in Vietnam

"While on guard duty; myself, three buddies, two
Vietnamese soldiers and two kids were talking. We were

sitting down on the side of a dirt highway when a six by (a heavy duty truck) hit a landmine. The force of the explosion pushed us all out of the way. Just then the six by ended up back in the area were we were sitting. Had we not been thrown by the blast we would have been hit or even killed. As it was, I was thrown into a ditch. I had many lacerations on my arms and back. The truck driver was saved by the 3/4 plate underneath the truck. For this incident I received the Purple Heart."

JOSEPH L. MEINERS

Branch of Service:
  U.S. Army
Years of Service:
  3 years, 27 months   WWII
Outfit:
  962 Engineer Maintenance Company
Areas Stationed:
  England, France, Belgium, Germany
Ships:
  Traveled overseas on the Queen Mary
Specialty:
  Emergency Repair Mechanic

"We traveled overseas to England in December of 1943, and crossed the English Channel to France on June 6, 1944. Our intended duty was beach maintenance and the repair of equipment, although, my partner and I ended up as medics stretcher-bearers for several days.

I stayed on the front lines through the entire war. I lost two helpers from small arms fire. I was in the hospital twice and one time I was close to death. This happened during the Battle of the Bulge. I was rendered deaf and blind for two weeks. I was sent back to the front lines before I was fully recovered; I still could not hear or see. There, halfway between the American and German lines I did manage to repair a tractor.

After the Battle of the Bulge, we quickly moved on to meet the Russians on the Elbe River. After the end of the war, we traveled back to Belgium for a short time and then on to La Harre, France to ship back to the United States. I was discharged in November of 1945."

Joseph Meiners, July 2005

RUDY MEISL

Branch of Service:
    U.S. Air Force
Years of Service:
    4 years   Korean War
Outfit:
    91st Recon
Areas Stationed:
    Okinawa, Tachikava, Yokota Air Bases
Aircraft:
    Superfortress, B-29, B-50, B-36
Specialty:
    Radio and Intercommunication in the aircraft and
    repair on the flight line and in the shop.

"The four years that I spent in the service were a positive phase in my life. The Air Force gave me the opportunity to see certain parts of the world from the ground and from the air. The Air Force also sent me to Radio School, which came in handy when I applied for a job in the commercial field.

I personally was not involved in any direct conflict, but did see one of our planes crash just prior to landing on the runway.

In the electronic field, in that era, transistors and IC's were years away. Tubes were the primary electronics in those days."

GEORGE D. MILLER Jr.

Branch of Service:
    U.S. Marine Corps   (Sergeant)
Years of Service:
    July 1950 to December 1970 (Korea and Vietnam)
Outfits:
    Weapons Company, 2nd Battalion, 5th Marine
        Regiment, 1st Marine Division
    Weapons Company, 3rd Battalion, 4th Marine
        Regiment, 3rd Marine Division
Areas Stationed:
    United States (West and East Coast); Korea; Okinawa;
        Japan; Vietnam
Specialty:
    Flamethrower Operator

"I worked in several different fields over my 20-years in
the Marine Corps. When I went into the Korean War,
everyone that could go was going. If you were under 18-
years old, you were not allowed in a combat zone. Since I
was only 17 at the time, I was sent to San Francisco and was
assigned guard duty at the Supply Depot. When I turned 18,
I received combat training at Camp Pendleton, California. I
was then assigned to a weapons company and trained in an
Anti-tank platoon. This platoon included anti-tank rockets,
demolitions and flamethrowers. We were trained in all three
areas. When I arrived in Korea, September 1951, I was
assigned to Weapons Company, 2nd Battalion, 5th Marines
Regiment, 1st Marines Division. I was assigned as a Flame-
thrower Operator for 9-months, then promoted to Sergeant
and made a squad leader.

I was sent back to the United States in November of 1952, and I was assigned to Weapons Company, 3rd Battalion, 4th Regiment, 3rd Marine Division. I was the Platoon Sergeant of the Anti-Tank Platoon and the squad leader.

In 1953, I was transferred to Treasure Island in San Francisco, California. I was assigned as a prison guard until 1956.

I then went into data processing. This was before computers, and all the accounting was done on mechanical IBM machines. I worked as a machine operator until 1959. The Marine Corps wanted an accounting platoon in the combat units, but IBM would not send their own repairmen into a combat zone. The USMC sent thirteen of us to IBM schools for training as repairmen. I was lucky and was selected. When computers started replacing the mechanical machines, we were trained on them also.

In 1965, I went to Vietnam. When I came back in 1966, I was assigned to a data processing unit in North Carolina. After 18-months, I was sent to San Diego, California, and then 10-months later sent to the Marine Corps Air Station at El Toro, California.

I retired from the Marines in 1970. Because of my training, I went to work for IBM only 2-days after my military retirement. I worked for several other companies before moving to Northern California and retiring for good."

ROBERT "BOB" MINOR

Branch of Service:
  U.S. Marine Corps
Years of Service:
  2-years   Korean War
Outfit:
  Baker 1/1/1
Areas Stationed:
  All over North and South Korea (2 times)
Specialty:
  Machine Guns (light 30's), grunt

HORSE SHOE RIDGE
by: Bob Minor

It had never happened before but we were in the reserves. The Marine Corp will never, never let you sleep. So, of course, we saddled up and moved out. As we started north, we ran into the whole South Korean Army on the run going south. They had, as usual, thrown away everything but their chow and deserted their lines in force.

I had lost my fifth carbine, so I had no choice but to wait until I spotted a Slope with a nice weapon running right by me. I tripped him, grabbed his rifle and gear, and was ready to play war again. At that time, I had no idea how badly I was going to need his brand new toys and gear!

After a while, we came into view of the biggest mountain in Korea, and as you can guess, that was the one we had to take! Many long hours later, we were almost to the top. Then, before we knew what was happening, the bad guys came right over the ridge and we ran. We made it down with only a few minor casualties and started up the next one. However, by then we could see millions of Gooks on the hills around us. They were everywhere, completely surrounding us on all sides. By the time we started digging in, we were beat; and I do mean beat!

One strange thing was that the BAR (Browning Automatic Rifle) man next to us had a clear field of fire through the woods and we had absolutely NONE. So, we carved out a 7-inch deep hole and loaded magazines for him until dark. A few hours later, we awoke to a continuous stream of blue and green Gook tracer's right over us and our 7-inch hole.

There was an exchange going on between our mortars and theirs. Then, their tracers found our mortar men. Some of our machine gunners joined in and it really looked like the Forth of July! There were red, white, blue and green tracers ricocheting every which way. It was a long night to say the very least!

About dawn, our Lieutenant, Ed Dibble, ordered withdrawal. Everything started out smoothly, with us backing down the hill, firing uphill and holding them off pretty good. Then, all of a sudden, all hell broke loose! The trees started exploding from all the small arms fire coming in from every direction, and right in the middle of this, some brave Lieutenant, leading a column of men carrying some wounded on stretchers went right across an open rice paddy! And the Slopes let him go! He was one brave man! The noise was horrific with trees, ground, and everything exploding on all sides of us. Dibble yelled, "Drop everything and get!" At the same time, a burst got Joe Miller through the horns and me through the leg. About then it was as if someone was yelling "Broward" over a P.A. system, over and over. I knew then that something really bad had happened to my best cruddy buddy. I flopped down, dropped my pack, and reloaded to take off again. In those few seconds, everyone around me was gone. And I mean GONE! I was all alone and scared. I spotted a ditch running perpendicular to the road down below and foolishly, I headed towards it. I jumped in and found it full of dead Marines; about twenty of them! The incoming fire never slackened so I tromped right over them and down to the road. I had no idea who they were or what outfit they were with.

About that time, two of our tanks came backing around the bend. They were putting out heavy fire up into the hills. I broke and ran for the closest one, got under it and started shooting at the Gooks crossing the road. Suddenly, I heard a noise from behind me and it was a BAR man from out of somewhere (I didn't know and didn't care). He was firing the other way at the Gooks crossing behind the tanks. The tank opened up with her 90, and I thought I had been hit by artillery, because the noise and dust clouds were so bad, so I decided to move on. I took off and never saw that BAR man again.

I finally made it down to a little stream and caught up with the rest of my outfit. Broward was still on my mind. He was a kid who was courageous and never afraid. I was always afraid!

Sergeant Brink came along and with his usual charm said, "Okay, Minor, quit trying to bleed to death and move out!" We worked our way to a spot where several machine guns were putting down cover fire while jeeps filled with the dead and wounded and moved out. A strange thing happened here, when out of nowhere there was a Gook in the middle of our gunners. Some Marine, better and faster than me, shot him down dead before I could even pull the trigger.

Our corpsman made me get on a jeep and away we went. We came around the bend and a Chinese group was crossing the road in front of us. Our driver was the world's greatest, and cut right down the side of a mountain. The jeep was dragging a trailer filled with dead and wounded on the hood and me right on top. The Slopes let us go right on past them!

Finally, we made it to a landing strip with one large tent of wounded on one side. I went in looking for Broward, but with no luck. I couldn't tell it, because he was so shot up in the face, but one of the wounded guys who was a close friend of Broward's learned that he did live through it! I found this out after all these years!

I was bandaging my leg when two lieutenants came and yelled, "We have room for one walking wounded." That was me. I was the last one on the last DC3. When the pilot got it turned around and was sitting there revving his engines, Chinese troops were crossing the runway on all sides of us. They just went right past the hospital tent and after a minute or so, a Chinese officer waved us off with his sword. Away we went again. Thank God! He just let us go! I have often wondered what happened to the lieutenants, doctors and the wounded we left there. I was thinking of Broward still and cried for them all.

In just a few minutes, we landed at Tague. Our fighter planes, jets and props were all coming in. The pilots had less than five minutes for fuel, food, ammunition and to reload. Then they were off again ready to fight! I stayed in the hospital in Tague until it fell. Then I was airlifted to Japan on another DC3. The plane was so full that the nurses were walking on the edge of stretchers. One Marine died on the way over to Japan. He just bled to death. He was on the top bunk so blood was all over the guys beneath him.

I still looked for Broward in five different hospitals in Japan on my way to Yokohama Naval Hospital. Every evening at about 5:00 P.M. the train would come in loaded with wounded and everyone turned out to meet it. We had an exceptionally long night working with the wounded, and I finally made it back to my ward about 3:00 A.M.

I was really close to cracking and sat on my bunk and started shaking all over. I was close to turning in my I.D. card. Then, in the dark, I heard a weak, sick voice. It was ole Broward right in the very next bunk! He had seen me in all those places, but was paralyzed and couldn't speak, until then! Broward had been hit by a machine gun and had a broken back. But, being much more of a Marine than I was, he went back to Korea. I was sent home because of the death of my brother.

Ed Dibble did a great job leading us out of that trap. There is no doubt that without him we would have been dead in that ditch too!

Joe Miller was wounded twice in the South Pacific during World War II, and once in Korea, but he came back again. Two Purple Hearts allow you to quit and go home! Unfortunately, his luck ran out that day at Horse Shoe.

Ron Broward has been back to Korea several times to try to find the bodies of Marines who never came home. Miller is still there. I tracked down Miller's family in New York for Broward. I called to tell them of Broward's great efforts and great expense, but they were not interested and we never heard back from them.

Oh, yes. On the way out, I came across a lieutenant who had been hit through the throat. He had several clamps holding him together. I stopped, held his hand and said a prayer for him. I was then ordered to get on the jeep. I heard many years later that he lived through it all, too. It wasn't his day for God to take him. I hope someday someone will read this and call me about the men in that tent just to know more about them and if they made it out.

While I was in the hospital in Japan, a beautiful girl got to meet me. She walked up to our bunks and said, "Hi. My name is Jennifer Jones, is there anything I can do for you?" I said, "No, but several badly burned Sailors came in yesterday and one really needs help." Their carrier had taken several hits off the coast of Korea and this one guy wasn't going to make it. That was until Jennifer got in his blackened and badly burned face and told him he was not going to die on her! She stayed with him and the next day he was up and around!

Broward spent five years in the hospital all because of that day on Horse Shoe Ridge. Rector, Reno, Howard and I all met at Bimbo's Chosin Few Reunion last year. It was the first time that we were all together again. I have seen many men at our Reunions and hope to see them again.

The final score on Horse Shoe that day: Over 650 Chinese dead and 38 Marines died.

NORMAN MATTHEW MOHAR

Branch of Service:
    U.S. Army (Sergeant)
Years of Service:
    2-13-43 to 10-19-45
Outfit:
    2nd Battalion, 30th Infantry Regiment of 3rd Division
Areas Stationed:
    Fort Lewis, Washington; Camp Roberts, California;
    Camp Howze, Texas
    Overseas to the European Theater of Operation
Ships:
    U.S.S. John S. Pillsbury (Troopship)
Specialty:
    A&P Platoon-Ammo and Demolitions; special
    Rifleman

    Mr. Mohar was an Infantryman during WWII. He served from the Casino Front, Anzio, Rome, South of France and all the way to Germany and Austria. He was awarded many medals for his distinguished service, two of which were the Bronze Star with a cluster and the Purple Heart.

    He earned the Soldier's Medal for heroism not involving actual conflict with the enemy. During river crossing maneuvers near Nancy, France, on the morning of March 10, 1945, Sergeant Mohar swam 25-yards into a swift river current to reach and rescue a drowning soldier. When the soldier fell into the water and lost control, he quickly weakened, went down twice and could only make feeble efforts to aid himself. Sergeant Mohar unhesitatingly leaped in the river, fully clothed, and after extreme exertions against the current and weight of his clothing, brought the drowning man to safety.

Mr. Mohar has recorded his amazing experiences on a web site. You can read his story by entering his full name in the "Google" search engine.

The rifleman fights without promise of either reward or relief. Behind every river there's another hill - and behind that hill, another river. After weeks or months in the line only a wound can offer him the comfort of safety, shelter, and a bed. Those who are left to fight, fight on, evading death but knowing that with each day of evasion they have exhausted one more chance for survival. Sooner or later, unless victory comes this chase must end on the litter or in the grave.

General Omar Bradley

KRISTA OCHS MUNYON

Branch of Service:
U.S. Army   (First Sergeant)
Years of Service:
1981 - 2004
Outfit:
331st Army Security Agency Battalion;
165th Military Intelligence Battalion (TE);
1st Military Intelligence Battalion (AE);
2nd Armored Division (Hell on Wheels);
3rd Infantry Division (Rock of the Marne);
4th Infantry Division (Iron Horse);
66th MI Brigade;
The National Security Agency;
10th Special Forces Group;
Office for the Chairman of the Joint Chiefs of staff;
The Intelligence and Security Command (INSCOM)
Liaison and Detachment First Sergeant;
Operations Sergeant of Field Station Korea;
Headquarters First Sergeant-527th MI Battalion
Areas Stationed:
Karlsruhe, Germany; Wiesbaden, Germany; Fort
Hood, Texas; Wuerzburg, Germany; Augsburg,
Germany; Fort Carson, Colorado; Fort Meade,
Maryland; Stuttgart, Germany; the Pentagon,
Washington, DC; Fort Huachuca, Arizona; Field
Station Korea (Camp Humphries)
Specialty:
Russian and Serbo-Croatian linguist in the Electronic
Warfare Signals Intelligence Field (SIGINT)-Military
Intelligence Corps.

"As you can see, for us 'lifers'- we move from assignment to assignment every couple of years and have the opportunity to work with many types of units. I served during a very transitional time for the Army, we went from the era of the Cold War, a very important time for intelligence personnel, to what we now call Stability and Support Operations, or small-scale, counter-insurgency warfare.

My conflicts were, of course, the Cold War (as a Russian linguist), and then later Desert Shield/Desert Storm, two deployments to the Balkans (Yugoslavia/Bosnia/Kosovo), the 'new' cold war in Korea, and of course, the Global War on Terrorism (Afghanistan and later, Iraq). The operational tempo for the average soldier today is much higher than it was many years ago.

The first memories deal with children in places where life is very bad. We are so fortunate in America to have what we have and when you get to go to a place where life is not that way, it stays with you forever. When I was in Sarajevo, I had two children (a little boy about four and a little girl about seven) beg me through my vehicle window for water. Water was scarce and pretty strictly watched over, but I had a fresh bottle in my back seat and I gave it to them. They were so excited...about water! An officer that was out from Ilidza (our base) with me, chided me for giving away the water but I did not argue with him. I knew in my heart I could pass over a bottle of water from my own ration to give it to them. How could I look them in the eyes and say 'no'? They haunt me and I often wonder what happened to them - they must be grown by now.

I have two other memories of Yugoslavia. The first deals with my own fear and the sheer adrenalin rush of being sniped at and of walking inadvertently into an unmarked minefield. My Muslim translator, Muki, talked me out of the minefield and when I came out, all I could do was sit on the road. In retrospect, it was as if time got very, very slow for a moment - as if everything was happening underwater. It was undoubtedly one of the most intense moments of my life. My lieutenant was wounded in the neck by a sniper and the time effect thing was the same. Everything went in slow motion. One moment he was standing and talking to a gentleman in downtown Sarajevo and the next moment he was hollering and on the ground. We were even more scared after driving quickly from the area when we realized how close he had come to being killed. We figured that the sniper had what we call a 'bead' (the target) on his head and fate intervened and made him turn at probably the exact time the sniper squeezed the trigger, thus creasing him in the neck. He was awarded the Purple Heart.

When I worked in Yugoslavia, I worked with issues related to the genocidal war crimes of that time. My other memory of that time is the smell and look of many bodies in a mass grave. No words can adequately describe it - to this day I am haunted by the women who were at the fringes of the sites like this, looking for their lost husbands, fathers, sons...I was ashamed to look at them, if only because I am a human being and human beings owe it to each other not to inflict such horror on each other. The smell...oh...enough about that.

There are so many other things I could tell you about my experiences. During Desert Storm, my memories are of no sleep and a lot of guard duty. In Korea, it was the unbelievable cold of winter and intense, muggy heat of summer and monsoon.

I remember at the Pentagon one night when we were bombing Yugoslavia, listening to a female Major say goodnight to her three little daughters on the phone next to me. Then there was a pause and I could tell she was a little embarrassed and then she cupped her hand over the phone and very softly started singing, 'Rock-a-Bye Baby' to her little girls. Here was a woman that was responsible for targeting places for bombs, reporting information to the President of the United States, but in that moment, she was just a mommy and she was so tender with her children that night. I will never forget that.

However, the biggest thing I want to share with you is my experience as a First Sergeant, and what I think the greatest thing about the military is - the soldier. We soldiers are a family. As a 'top' I had to tell them when members of their families were sick, dying or dead; hold their hands when they were sick; take care of them; get them out of jail and discipline them when they got into trouble; help them achieve success; and help them through divorces, fear, fatigue and all the other things that life presents but is so much harder when you are so very far from home and alone apart from your fellow soldiers. I myself had sergeants and soldiers that helped me through the hardest times of my life, the loss of my son and the loss of my father. Without their support, even with my husband, I am not sure I could have made it myself. I thank God for them.

I will carry my soldiers with me for the rest of my life - the look in their eyes when they complete something they never thought they could accomplish, their own little personal victories. The sorrow in their eyes when they lose someone they care about. Their joys when they have a child, are promoted, or receive a medal - so very proud. They are the best our nation has - they give everything they have and then some. They endure more than any civilian can ever imagine, heat, cold, hunger, filth, fatigue, boredom, adrenalin – you name it. If someone were to ask me what military life is like, I would describe these things to them and tell them that life in the military is a life of extremes, and it takes people of extreme devotion to execute our myriad tasks."

Mrs. Munyon retired as a First Sergeant in August of 2004. Her last assignment was in the Republic of Korea. She now teaches soldiers to fly unmanned aerial vehicles at Fort Huachuca, Arizona.

DIANE MURDOCK

Branch of Service:
    U.S. Marine Corps
Years of Service:
    1961 - 1965   Vietnam
Outfit:
    VMA 211 (Marine Jet Fighter Squadron)
Areas Stationed:
    MCRD, Parris Island, South Carolina
    MCAS, El Toro, California
    MCB, Camp Pendleton, California
Specialty:
    Jet Engine Mechanic - Ground Support

"During the Vietnam era, the opportunities for women were very limited. My most enjoyable duty was driving the reserves around for three months at Camp Pendleton, California.

Now I am the Commander of the American Legion Post 234 at Mountlake Terrace, Washington."

MICHAEL A. NAIMO

Branch of Service:
   U.S. Navy
Years of Service:
   1967 - 1971   Vietnam
Areas Stationed:
   Homeport while in the U.S. - Port Chicago, California
   Three WestPac Cruises - Homeport while abroad -
      Subic Bay, Philippine Islands
Ships:
   U.S.S. Paricutin AE-18 (Ammunition Ship)
Specialty:
   Boatswain's Mate 2nd Class

"I spent all of my enlistment aboard the U.S.S. Paricutin.
Our ship was an ammunition ship named after a volcano in
Mexico. Our mission during the Vietnam conflict was to
supply other ships such as, aircraft carriers, battleships,
heavy cruisers, destroyers, and any other ship, with ammo.
We would take up station away from the battles and wait for
the ships to call in their order for ammunition. We would
then get the required ammo out of its storage area and up on
deck. My job was to make sure the required rigging was set
up on the proper station for the ship. The ship would then
pull up along side of us approximately 65-feet away and we
would transfer the ammo over to them using different types
of transfer rigs. The rigs consisted of wenches, cables,
pulleys, hooks and slings. The most rewarding part of my
cruises was when a patrol boat that was patrolling the rivers
called in an order for some ammo. Upon completion of the
transfer, the skipper of the patrol boat asked our Captain if

we had any ice cream. We gave them two containers of ice cream. The expression on the faces of the crew on the patrol boat was that of pure joy. I would have never guessed that ice cream would make someone that happy. I will always remember their faces that day.

The most terrifying experience I had while serving aboard the U.S.S. Paricutin was during our last cruise in 1970. We were caught in Typhoon Joan while on station, and it sure made a mess of our ship. We had ammunition break loose in our #4-cargo hole and it rolled from side to side with the rolling of the ship in the heavy seas. Many people thought that the ship would not make it out of the storm. Someone was watching over us those days."

KARL NEWELL

Branch of Service:
U.S. Army
Years of Service:
March 1966 - December 1968
Vietnam: May 1967 - December 1968
Outfit:
536th Engineer Company (PC)
Areas Stationed:
Qui Nhon, South Vietnam
Specialty:
Building of dock facilities and bridges

"Our company provided support for the 45th Engineer Group. In addition to building docks in the harbor at Qui-Nhon, We maintained roads and repaired bridges on Highway 1, from Tui Hua in the South of Qui Nhon to Bong-Son and An Khe North of Qui Nhon. I was in Qui Nhon during the 1968 Tet Offensive."

KENNETH EARL NORRIS

Branch of Service:
    U.S. Army   (Corporal)
Years of Service:
    3 years, 3 months   WWII
Outfit:
    33rd Division, Company E
Areas Stationed:
    Hawaii, New Guinea, Philippines, Japan
Specialty:
    Rifleman

Mr. Norris traveled with his outfit to the South Pacific by way of Hawaii. They fought in many areas from Australia to the Philippines. At one point during the fighting, Mr. Norris received shrapnel in his leg. It was never removed, so he still carries it around today.

Next, they were sent to Japan. Mr. Norris was the lead jeep off the ship, drove right off into a shell hole, and had to swim out. Divers pulled the jeep out, oiled, cleaned, dried it and drove it on to the Headquarters in Japan.

One of the highlights of Mr. Norris' time in the South Pacific was standing on a secured beach and watching as General Douglas Mac Arthur waded to shore on his return to the Philippines.

Mr. Norris finally returned home in November of 1945.

JOSEPH R. OLTMAN

Branch of Service:
> U.S. Army

Years of Service:
> 1966 - 1968 Vietnam

Outfit:
> Charley Company 3/7, 199th Light Infantry Brigade

Areas Stationed:
> Mekong Delta, Vietnam

Aircraft:
> Hughie and Chinook helicopters

Specialty:
> Air Mobile Infantry

"We landed in South Vietnam on Christmas day of 1966. Some N.C.O. dressed as Santa Clause came out to meet us in a jeep, welcoming us to Vietnam.

We operated mostly in jungle or rice patty country. We moved in and out of areas mostly by helicopter, but sometimes we would go up the Mekong River by river patrol boat. We ran search and destroy missions during the day, and ambushes at night. Most of the search and destroy operations were company size and the night ambushes were squad size. We started with 10-12 men in a squad. By the time I was promoted to Squad Leader (About 5 months into my tour) we were down to 6-7 men per squad. The first man killed in my company was my Platoon Leader. He died because of a booby-trapped 105 mm artillery round. We suffered many of our casualties from booby-traps and snipers or when the Viet Cong or the North Vietnam Army ambushed us. These memories are almost 40-years old, but

217

they are still very fresh.

As a returning Vietnam Veteran at the San Francisco airport, I was spat at and called 'Baby Killer' by a group of protestors. For 35-years, the only 'Welcome Home' I received was from my Mom and Dad. For all those years, I hid the fact that I had been in combat in Vietnam and avoided any discussion about it. For 35-years, I felt I had done something wrong by answering when my country called me. Those protestors seemed to have forgotten the price of the freedoms we all enjoy."

CARL E. PARKS

Branch of Service:
   U.S. Marine Corps
Years of Service:
   3 1/2 years WWII
Outfit:
   'M' Battery, 4th Battalion, 10th Regiment, 2nd Marine
   Division
Areas Stationed:
   New Caledonia, Guadalcanal, Tarawa, Saipan, Tinian,
   Okinawa and Occupation of Japan
Ships:
   APA Ship Hensdale #120
   (Thirteen different Transports and Troop Ships)
Specialty:
   Radio Operator and Forward Observer for Artillery

The Longest and Scariest Day of My Life
by Carl E. Parks

April 1, 1945, I had just eaten breakfast and was eating an
apple in the dark out room between the interior and exterior
door when a blast from bombs exploded in the engine
rooms.

I said to myself, "We've hit another ship or something." I
rushed outside onto the port deck, heard a loud swishing
sound, went to the rail, looked over and there about 40 feet
aft and maybe 20 feet below me was a big hole with water
rushing in at a terribly fast rate.

A Kamikaze plane actually went through a portion of the
mess hall that I had recently vacated and went into the

engine rooms; I say rooms because it destroyed both engine rooms, and the water was going into three compartments of a seven-compartment ship. I have heard that flooding four compartments would sink the ship immediately.

The ship began to list immediately to the port side. Everyone scrambled up to the starboard side and the ship's personnel began trying to lower the lifeboats. It was quite difficult because of the list, which I thought was more than 13 degrees, as I had to go from port side to starboard with my hands on the deck, it was so steep. However, by all hands on the starboard side and the able crews working below, the ship settled back somewhat and I was able to go below and gather up some of my personal belongings.

After sometime, they were able to lower the boats and as the word was passed to disembark, I got the word from my Battery Commander that I was to stay aboard with my radio jeep, which was to be taken off by another ship along side later on that day.

Well, that was the second time that day my heart sank. I wanted to go with my buddies, but I stacked my gear top side and settled in to help the others disembark.

There actually was a time that my memory just quit working. I remember seeing smoke everywhere and other ships being hit by Kamikaze planes and bombs. One LST I was looking at about a quarter mile off the rear must have been carrying lots of ammunition, because it just completely disappeared in a blast, hardly anything floated after the smoke settled.

I found a place near the rear on the main deck and settled in for the worst day of my life, before or since. Remember, I knew no one aboard because, other than the ships crew and the other Marines aboard, (I only saw about 30) were from other units, mostly the drivers of other radio jeeps, ambulance jeeps, and one-tons. There was one tank with a blade for covering ammunition fires etc.

I was sitting near a 20mm anti-aircraft gun, when a sailor asked me to help him with the ammo, etc. I spent the rest of the day with him and we operated the gun all day. I did not get his name, if I even asked, I have forgotten.

We sat there dead in the water until about 2 P.M. when a smaller ship came, I have since learned was, Leo (AKA-6). It seemed to me to be smaller than an LST. However, it hooked on to us and towed us about 20-miles to Kerama Retto Harbor where there were numerous ships of all sizes that had been hit by Kamikaze planes or damaged by bombs or shellfire. One was a cruiser where a bomb went down the stack. That was one long and miserable trip, enemy planes were flying over all day and I guess we were not a #1 priority, because they passed us by looking for undamaged or bigger targets.

We did not get into the harbor that day. Just before dark, a submarine net tender began stringing a net across the entrance to the harbor and the tow ship, Leo, dropped us like a hot potato and beat it into the harbor ahead of the net tender. That was the third time that day that my heart sunk another 3 inches.

Just about dusk, two enemy planes tried to finish us off. Fortunately, they had expended their bombs but circled and were making a run at us to either torpedo or just strafe us, I don't know which, but with the help of a lot of fire power coming from inside the (protected submarine harbor) we were firing every gun on our ship that would work without electric power. Our luck was still holding as both planes were hit and tumbled into the water less than 600 yards from our ship.

As I said before, that was the worst day of my life. I

remember it started at 0600. The loudspeaker was announcing the time when the plane hit us and the power went dead. Up until that time, everything had been fine. I had slept well and gotten up about 0515 and ate a good breakfast (do not ask me what it was). We were scheduled to land on Okinawa. I didn't know or don't remember hearing that we were to make a feint landing off the east coast of Okinawa to draw the enemy away from where the actual landing first took place on the west side. That feint drew a lot of attention by the Kamikaze planes.

Back to the longest and scariest day and the longest night, I guess you know there was no sleeping that night. I cannot say it was without entertainment. The sky was lit up most of the night with anti-aircraft fire from the Hinsdale and all the other ships in the harbor. I have never seen a 4th of July that would come close to equaling the display of lights over Kerama Retto Island the night of April 1, 1945. April Fools Day? My eye, it was for real.

The next morning, when they opened the nets something came out and towed us in, I do not remember what, because the minute they hooked on I fell asleep at my gun. When I woke up, we were tied up to the U.S.S. Pitt, APA 223, another ship that had been hit but was better off than the Hinsdale.

We all were put on a work party to unload oranges. Thousands of crates, and I do not ever remember getting oranges for breakfast.

Finally, I would like to hear from some of the fellows who experienced that awful day. Especially the Navy guy that showed me how to fire and load a 20mm anti-aircraft gun, aft on the starboard side.

I think we should have a reunion of those courageous veterans left on this wonderful earth.

GARY R. PERKINS

Branch of Service:
    U.S. Navy
Years of Service:
    1952 - 1956 Korean War
Outfit:
    Air Dale
Areas Stationed:
    NAS Sandpoint, Seattle, Washington
    NAS Atsugi, Japan
Ships:
    U.S.S. Hornet CVA-12 (Task Force 77 - 7th Fleet)
Specialty:
    Air Operations and Turret Gunner

Mr. Perkins served aboard the U.S.S. Hornet during the Korean War. He worked with many different aircraft including the F4U Corsair, F8F Bearcat, TBF Avenger and the PBY Seaplanes. He served on the aircrew and was a plane captain. His squad made C.O.D. flights to all the carriers in the 7th fleet. These were the special flights for security mail to all the ships of the fleet, certain land positions, and to the Generals on mainland Korea.

"I did nothing special; I just did a job like everyone else. I never got a scratch...it was no big deal. I lost my best friend, E.G. Mount, in a flight deck crash. He was a real hero, best of the best!"

GORDON PETRIE

Branch of Service:
  U.S. Army (Captain)
Years of Service:
  April 1941 - December 1946 WWII
Outfit:
  Signal Corps, Anti-Aircraft, General's Aide-de-Camp,
  Army Security Agency
Areas Stationed:
  Fort Monmouth, New Jersey; Boston, Massachusetts;
  Hicksville, Long Island, New York; New Guinea;
  Philippine Islands; China; Korea; Japan; Australia;
  Okinawa
Specialty:
  "In the beginning my specialty was in the field of
  RADAR, an acronym for RAdio Detecting And
  Ranging, this was a hush, hush area in the early
  1940's. I branched out with different assignments."

"My experiences are from a time period before television,
before cell phones, and before satellites orbiting the globe.
Morse Code, semaphoring, and coded materials were the
backbone of communications. Radar was a big advance. I
had a radar repair team with one officer and four highly
skilled sergeants. We traveled all over New Guinea and the
Philippines to keep the radar links open. We used a 3/4-ton
truck, a maintenance truck, (essentially a mobile repair
shop), a diesel/electric generator truck, and I secured a jeep
at each post.

  There is no connection between my first overseas
assignment with the radar repair team and my last

assignment with the ASA (Army Security Agency, forerunner to the National Security Agency), except that both involved special knowledge and much secrecy. Every military assignment has its own protocols and rules.

In between the first and last, I served with an Anti-Aircraft unit and as a general's aide. The aide-de-camps were under the jurisdiction of the Judge Advocate General (JAG). Each assignment was part of the greater effort of all our armed forces; the truck drivers, the medical corps, the engineers, the cooks, the maintenance teams, etc. It took the combined efforts of everyone in whatever job he or she had to win the war against Germany and Japan and to allow us to return home. My generation (I am in my 80's) believed in duty, honor, sacrifice, hard work and patriotism. And when it was over, we went home to pick up the pieces of an interrupted life and worked toward our futures."

RICHARD M. PIATT

Branch of Service:
U.S. Navy
Years of Service:
1944 - 1947 (+4 years in Reserve Status)
Outfit:
"Rover" Destroyer Squadron
Areas Stationed:
North Island Naval Air Station, San Diego,
California; Treasure Island, San Francisco,
California; and several ships
Ships:
U.S.S. Halford (DD480); U.S.S. Yarnell (DD541);
U.S.S. St. Croix (APA231); U.S.S. Boxer (CV21)
Specialty:
3rd Class Petty Officer; Quartermaster and Signalman

Mr. Piatt served aboard the U.S.S. Halford, which was
involved in many different operations such as Bismarck
Archipelago, Marianas, Western Caroline Islands, Leyte and
Luzon. It was also part of the capture and occupation of
Saipan and Guam, and the consolidation of the Northern
Solomon Islands.

Mr. Piatt remembers a time in the Philippines when a
Japanese suicide pilot tried to bomb and ram into their ship.
They shot him down with their anti-aircraft guns.
Somehow, the pilot survived and they found him sitting on
the wing of his fighter plane, floating on the ocean. They
transferred him to a cruiser for information gathering.

In the Leyte Gulf Battle area, Mr. Piatt witnessed
hundreds of Japanese survivors floating in an oil and fuel

slick in the water. They all perished because they would not surrender.

After leaving the U.S.S. Boxer, Mr. Piatt was assigned to shore patrol as a Military Policeman in San Francisco, California. His service on the U.S.S. Yarnell, U.S.S. St. Croix and U.S.S. Boxer were all during peacetime.

Mr. Piatt earned many medals and citations for his service: The American Campaign, Asiatic Pacific Campaign (7 Battle Stars), The Philippine Liberation (2 Battle Stars), Occupation Service-Japan, WWII Victory Medal and the Philippine Republic Presidential Unit Citation.

JAMES E. PRATT

Branch of Service:
   U.S. Army (Special Forces)
   Central Intelligence Agency
   Blackwater (Independent Contractor)
Years of Service:
   U.S. Army: (23 years total service)
       Cold War, Central America, Grenada, Bosnia
       First Gulf War, Invasion of Iraq
   Central Intelligence Agency: 5 years of service
   Blackwater: still working
Outfits:
   U.S. Army:
       1st Battalion, 7th Special Forces Group - Airborne
       1st Battalion, 19th Special Forces Group - Airborne
       2nd Battalion, 20th Special Forces Group - Airborne
   Central Intelligence Agency:
       Special Operations Branch, Department of
       Operations
   Blackwater:
       Protective Services Detail (Body Guard) in high
       threat areas
Areas Stationed:
   U.S. Army: worldwide
   Blackwater: Baghdad, AL-Hilla
Specialty:
   U.S. Army: 18E (Communications, Surveillance,
       Direction Finding, Satcom etc.)
       18C (explosives)
   Blackwater: Shooter of left rear seat follow car and
       follow car driver of a 3-car motorcade

In the U.S. Army, Mr. Pratt was a Staff Sergeant assigned to the ODA-055 (SCUBA Team). The team he was assigned to was tasked with several very interesting and high-risk missions.

During Mr. Pratt's time with the Central Intelligence Agency, he was assigned as Operations Officer. He received a high award and a bonus for a never before conducted mission. He was also commended for superior performance in providing critical communications support to the Secretary of State, Secretary of Defense, and to the Director of the CIA during their domestic travel.

Mr. Pratt went on to work as an independent contractor through a company called Blackwater. He was a Security Officer assigned to high threat areas such as Iraq, and was assigned to Protective Services Detail to the Department of State Diplomatic Security Services Group. His first assignment was to the newly opened American Consulate in AL-Hilla (about 90-miles South of Baghdad) to protect the Foreign Services Officers there. He was later moved up from shooter to follow car driver, responsible for the protection of the limo during the motorcade movement, and carried the shooters for the principle. He was later sent to Baghdad for the same position in the newly opened American Embassy.

During one assignment, Mr. Pratt was the driver of a follow car when they where attacked in a small town south of AL-Hilla. He had moved his vehicle in between the attacker and the limo he was protecting to give the limo driver time to get off the "X". Mr. Pratt was shot at numerous times, but had an excellent window in his vehicle, which stood up to the punishment and he was not hurt.

JOHN PRIBILA

Branch of Service:
>   U.S. Army (Sergeant)

Years of Service:
>   1987 - 1997
>>   (1990 to 1991: Gulf War)
>>   (1995 to 1996: Haiti)

Outfit:
>   Gulf War: 5/16 Infantry Battalion, 1st ID
>   (Big Red One)
>   Haiti: C Troop, 2nd Armored Cavalry

Areas Stationed:
>   Garlstedt, Germany; Fort Riley, Kansas; Wildflecken,
>   Germany; Baumholder, Germany; Fort Polk,
>   Louisiana; Fort Knox, Kentucky

Vehicles:
>   M3 Bradley Fighting Vehicle, HMWWV (Hummer)

Specialty:
>   Scout Recon

"I have served in many different units and went to many different schools. The absolute one thing that pops in my mind first is the cohesion and teamwork that prevails in any situation. I could not have accomplished anything without help from my fellow soldiers.

It is very hard to describe the most interesting facet of serving, which was war. It was a combination of fear, motivation, and not knowing exactly what to expect. I will never forget my first engagement in Iraq on a cold, wet night. Out of nowhere, several Russian made Iraqi BMP appeared. Due to superior training, my platoon did not panic. I was a gunner on my vehicle. We fired on the enemy and destroyed them. The rush of American superiority filled my veins. My entire career and life changed after that first shot. I was then a confirmed soldier and a man, doing what my uncles and grandfathers had done before me.

We lost several men in the war. One, which I was particularly close to, was Jeffrey Middleton. He was engaged by a friendly Apache Helicopter with Hellfire Missiles. Although hard to accept, it is part of war."

DANNY L. RIDER

Branch of Service:
> U.S. Navy (Master Chief Petty Officer)

Years of Service:
> February 1, 1951 to February 1, 1974
> Korean War, Cold War, Vietnam War

Outfit:
> Pacific Reserve Fleet; FASRON 117; FASRON 11;
> Special Weapons ("W") Division

Areas Stationed:
> San Diego, California; Long Beach, California;
> Barbers Point, Hawaii; Whidbey Island, Washington;
> Atsugi, Japan; Midway Island; Quonset Point, Rhode
> Island; Norfolk, Virginia; McAlester, Oklahoma

Ships:
> U.S.S. Isle Royale AD-29 (Destroyer Tender)
> U.S.S. Sperry AS-12 (Submarine Tender)
> U.S.S. Catfish SS-339 (Submarine)
> U.S.S. Kitty Hawk CVA-63 (Attack Aircraft Carrier)
> U.S.S. Lake Champlain CVS-39 (Anti-Submarine
>   Carrier)
> U.S.S. Intrepid CV-11 (Anti-Submarine Carrier)

Specialty:
> Torpedoman, Nuclear Weapons

"I joined the ROTC at my Boise, Idaho High School and as soon as I turned 17, I joined the U.S. Navy. I was sworn in on February 1, 1951, in Salt Lake City, Utah and reported to the U.S. Navy Training Center in San Diego, California. I finished boot camp and headed to my first duty station.

On the U.S.S. Isle Royale AD-29 in Long Beach,

California, we were tasked with putting some of the WWII Destroyers back into commission for the Korean War. At this time, I decided to become a Torpedo man's Mate, and my job was to prepare the torpedo tubes on the destroyers for use if needed. I did this work for two years and was promoted to Petty Officer Third Class. I was then sent to the U.S.S. Sperry AS-12 in San Diego, California.

On the U.S.S. Sperry, I was assigned to the steam torpedo shop assisting in the overhaul of torpedoes. I was sent to torpedo school in Newport, Rhode Island for formal training. When I returned from Newport, I went on leave, married my high school sweetheart and brought her to San Diego. I spent two years on the U.S.S. Sperry and advanced to Petty Officer Second Class. I was then transferred to NAS Barbers Point, Hawaii and spent two years assigned to the aerial steam torpedo shop.

Next, I was transferred to the Naval Air Station at Whidbey Island, Washington and was selected to undergo training to be a nuclear weapons man. I was sent to school in Key West, Florida and when I returned, I assumed my new duties in Nuclear Weapons. After two years at Whidbey Island, I transferred to submarine school in New London, Connecticut. Upon completion, I was assigned to the U.S.S. Catfish in San Diego.

Submarine duty was my one big mistake during my career. I found out that I was not cut out to be a submariner. Then fate smiled on me and a call was sent out for nuclear weapons trained personnel and I volunteered. I was transferred to Naval Air Station Atsugi, Japan for three years of duty in a nuclear weapons shop. We only had trainers, as our treaty with Japan forbade nuclear weapons on the soil. We maintained a readiness posture in case of possible war. The U-2's were stationed near our shop and when Gary Powers was shot down over Russia, our station went on alert due to the Japanese demonstrations outside our base. His plane may have come from our base and some Japanese were very upset. After about a week, everything calmed down and returned to normal.

At the end of my tour, I requested to officially change my rating to Nuclear Weapons Technician. I was sent to the Naval Training Center at Great Lakes, Illinois for Phase I training, which lasted for six weeks and then transferred to Sandi Base, Albuquerque, New Mexico for Phase II training, which was also six weeks. I finished each phase at #1 spot and was then transferred to the U.S.S. Kittyhawk CVA-63. It was in Yokosuka, Japan so I headed to Japan again to catch her.

Shortly after I reported aboard, we headed to the states. This was her maiden cruise as she was brand new. The day we crossed the International Dateline coming home, I was notified that I had made Chief Petty Officer. The Navy had just established two new pay grades, Senior Chief and Master Chief, but at that time, that was just a distant goal. When we got back to San Diego, I was sent to various schools to learn how to load nuclear weapons aboard all Navy aircraft capable of carrying them. After approximately six months, we had too many Chief Petty Officers and one was needed at Midway Island. I volunteered and once again was on my way to a new duty station.

My first view of Midway Island from the plane impressed me as being pretty small. It was about seven miles around and 12-feet above sea level. It turned out to be the best tour of duty in my 23-year naval career. I was the leading Chief Petty Officer in the nuclear weapons and torpedo shop. I was mainly doing administrative type work as well as taking care of the 20 men I was in charge of.

I had just finished 14-years in the Pacific areas of operations and wanted to see the European area. I put in a request to be transferred to the East Coast and was stationed at the Naval Air Station, Quonset point, Rhode Island. I boarded the U.S.S. Lake Champlain CVS-39, an anti-submarine aircraft carrier, which was scheduled to be decommissioned later in 1965. The short time I was aboard was a very exciting time. We were the primary recovery ship for the GT-5 pick-up of Conrad and Cooper after their suborbital flight. I did get to go to Bermuda on that trip. As soon as we returned to Quonset Point, I was transferred to the U.S.S. Intrepid CVS-11 operating out of Norfolk, Virginia. As soon as I went aboard, we headed to Guantanamo, Cuba for our workup prior to deploying to Vietnam. I had one day in port in Naples, Italy on our way through the Suez Canal to the Far East. We spent nine months off the coast of Vietnam while supporting the troops in country. After nine months, we headed back through the Suez Canal to our home in Norfolk and to our families. After two years on the U.S.S. Intrepid, I transferred to the Naval Ammunition Depot, McAlester, Oklahoma.

I was assigned to the Nuclear Weapons Inspection Team at McAlester and traveled all over the states and overseas inspecting nuclear capable sites. I was there only a short time, as instructors were needed at the Nuclear Weapons Training Center in San Diego, California. I volunteered and was sent to instructor school. After two years, I advanced in rate and was sent to the staff of Commander Cruiser Destroyer Forces Pacific. It was also in San Diego, so I did not have to move. I was there three years and once again, I advanced in rating to the top of the enlisted structure, Master Chief Petty Officer. I then transferred back to the Nuclear Weapons Training Center in San Diego, but this time as an Inspector. I worked at this duty for three years and was due to be transferred to Machrihanish, Scotland when I decided to retire. I had served twenty-three years and I was ready to settle down at last. I retired exactly twenty-three years to the date from when I enlisted."

DONALD P. RIDER

Branch of Service:
　　U. S. Navy Air Reserve
Years of Service:
　　4 years
Outfit:
　　Fashon, Dive Bomber Squadron
Areas Stationed:
　　Sand Point, Washington; San Diego, California;
　　Pensacola, Florida
Ships and Aircraft:
　　U.S.S. Saratoga and SB2C Helldiver
Specialty:
　　Rear Gunner

In 1943, my Uncle Don became a member of the Civil Air Patrol to get his pilots license. He took his first flight in an Air Force Piper Cub at the Bow Lake Airport, which is now Sea Tac Airport. His pilot training cost $35 per hour, which he earned by working two paper routes.

At the age of 17, he joined the Naval Air Reserve in Sand Point, Washington. He reported to Pensacola, Florida for flight training and later moved on to advanced flight school and received his JG rating.

"I had no engagement with the Japs. I did have to bail out of a twin engine aircraft over Sand Point, do to its rotor cables being caught."

GEORGE WELLINGTON RIDER
1895 - 1990

Branch of Service
U.S. Marine Corps
Years of Service:
WW I
Areas Stationed:
Quantico, Virginia and France
Specialty:
Message Carrier

In 1917, the war was imminent, so my Great Grandpa enlisted in the U.S. Marine Corps, much to his mother's dismay. She had always been opposed to war and the taking up of arms. Even so, he went off to Quantico, Virginia for boot camp. The Marine Corps would not accept his birth name of G. Wellington Rider. They insisted he have a "first" name, so the Marine Corps issued him the first name of George, which he carried to the end of his life.

He was immediately sent to France where he tried to honor his mother's wishes as much as possible by asking to be a motorcycle runner; this meant he would not have to take up arms. He was honored for his bravery in action by motoring across enemy lines in the middle of battles to alert the allies of important events.

Towards the end of the war, the Germans gassed the trenches and my Great Grandpa was right in the middle of it. He and another Marine were sent to Marseilles, in the south of France to recuperate.

During the time he was in Marseilles, the Armistice was declared on November 11, 1918 at 11:00 A.M. His buddy insisted they celebrate with a bottle of wine. My Great Grandpa got deathly ill and never touched another drop of alcohol for the rest of his life.

For his bravery during the war, my Great Grandpa earned many awards. One of which was the Purple Heart for being gassed, and another was the Croix de Guerre. This is a French military award for heroism in battle. He was never very proud of these awards because of the horrific memories they brought back. For years after the war, he woke up in the middle of the night, ringing wet with sweat, from the horrible nightmares he had.

The recipients of the Croix de Guerre were offered a year
of college in Europe, at either the University of Heidelberg
or the University of Edinburgh. He did not want to have
anything more to do with Germany, so he chose Scotland.
When he returned stateside, he attended the University of
Illinois, and then worked at General Electric before joining
the phone company.

HOWARD D. RIDER

Branch of Service:
    U.S. Navy
Years of Service:
    4 years - Naval Reserve
Outfit:
    Destroyer
Areas Stationed:
    Treasure Island and San Diego, California
Ships:
    U.S.S. Mansville
Specialty:
    Store Keeper

Me and my Uncle Howard,   August 2005

My Uncle Howard served in the Naval Reserves during the peacetime between the Second World War and the Korean War. His rank was Seaman 3rd class. His duty aboard the U.S.S. Mansville was as Store Keeper.

RALPH W. RIDER

Branch of Service:
    U.S. Air Force   (SSgt.)
Years of Service:
    1950 - 1954   Korean War
Areas Stationed:
    South Pacific, Japan, Korea, Europe
Ships and Aircraft:
    U.S.S. General Butner,
    T-33 trainer, C-47, DC-3, Transports 117 and C-97
Specialty:
    Airborne Electronics and Supply Specialist

Germany

My Grandpa was 21-years old at the time he entered the

245

Air Force. It was the last part of 1950, and the draft was in effect for the Korean War.

My Grandpa took his basic training at Lackland Air Force Base in Texas. It was mid-summer and the temperatures were 125-degrees during the day, and around 90-degrees at night. He found these temperatures difficult to get used to since they were so much different than his home in Seattle, Washington.

He then went to Biloxi, Mississippi for special training in Airborne Electronics and Supply Management.

His assignments took him to different areas in the South Pacific, Japan, Korea, and Europe.

His duties were shipping and handling of Airborne Radar Equipment and working in the supply department. During the four-years he spent in the Air Force, he rose to the rank of SSgt.

JOHN L. ROSS

Branch of Service:
> U.S. Navy

Years of Service:
> 1944 - 1946 WWII
> 1950 - 1952 (Air Navy Division)

Outfit:
> U.S.S. Saratoga CV3

Areas Stationed:
> Bremerton, Washington; South Pacific; Hunters
> Point, California

Ships:
> U.S.S. Saratoga, U.S.S. Prinston, U.S.S. Hornet,
> U.S.S. Iowa

Specialty:
> Catapult

When Mr. Ross was 12-years old, he visited his uncle in Port Orchard, Washington. They made the short trip to Bremerton to see the Navy ships docked in the yard. He was able to go aboard the U.S.S. West Virginia, U.S.S. Tennessee and the U.S.S. Saratoga. He was so impressed with what he saw, that he decided that he was going to join the Navy someday. Little did he know, in just a few years he would be a crewmember on the U.S.S. Saratoga and the world would be at war.

After finishing high school, in 1944, Mr. Ross enlisted in the Navy, went through boot camp at Farragut, Idaho and was sent to Bremerton to be assigned to the Saratoga.

The U.S.S. Saratoga had just returned to Bremerton after being heavily damaged in the Iwo Jima Invasion. It sustained three hours of aerial attack, five Kamikaze hits, and seven bomb hits. It had a forty-foot hole on the starboard quarter, which flooded out one of the boiler rooms. After all the repairs were finished, a shakedown cruise out of Bremerton was made. They were firing test rounds from the guns into the Puget Sound, when a projectile went off in one of the barrels and killed six men in the turret and blinded and badly burned six more men in the handling room. A speed run was made back to Bremerton for repairs and then it was off to Pearl Harbor.

"The greatest hazard aboard the ship was dodging our own aircraft. Two fellows who went to high school together and lived on the same block back in their hometown, went home on Survivor Leave to marry their high school sweethearts in a double wedding. Back aboard the ship, they both became tail-hook men to earn their flight skins, which meant a twenty percent raise in pay. This was a very dangerous job. The tail-hook men had to run on deck after an airplane caught the wire, let the plane coast backward and then free the landing wire from the tail-hook. One day a F6F came in for a landing with 120-gallons of 120-octane fuel still in the belly tank. (For some reason the pilot did not or could not use the fuel up before landing). It was a normal landing until about mid ship, the plane caught the third wire and the belly tank tore loose and went through the prop. Everything aft turned into a giant fireball. In the middle of this were the two tail-hook men. One was killed instantly and the other only made it through the night. The pilot made it out with only facial and hand burns. That was probably one of the worst accidents we had.

We occasionally had some comic relief. One night we were landing TBF's, when one came in low on fuel. We could hear the engine sputtering on the final approach. The pilot had to try to make the flight deck because if the engine quit, he would crash into the stern of the ship. When he made it to the deck, the aircraft was in a stalled out attitude, the engine quit just before the signalman gave him the cut. He stretched his glide and hit belly first on the ramp. The airplane broke in two just behind the ball turret and went down the deck on it's nose with it's tail in the air. The gunner in the ball turret had his feet sticking out and was looking at the stars, the tail went into the ocean. We, the crash crew, went up on a pallet on a fork lift to extract him. I grabbed hold of his hand and said, "You're OK! You're OK!" There was just no way he was going to let go. We had to cut his harness and pry his fingers loose before we could lift him onto the fork truck. I imagine anyone who just experienced something like that would be real shook up.

Up at the catapult end, the planes were being brought up on deck to be launched. As the Directors spotted the planes to the catapult, they would always make sure they were able to see the pilots face, this way they knew the pilot could see them. One time as a plane was being spotted, the pilot must have looked down to adjust something in the cockpit, because he missed the last Director and went past the place where we spot the plane into the catapult track. At that point, the pilot's only salvation was to give it throttle and try to fly it off. The track was only 76-feet long and we had a wind of about 25-knots coming over the bow. Because of this, his wheels were very light and there was no way he could stop. He would need about 90-mph speed to make it off the deck. Therefore, he gave it throttle and at the last 50 to 60-feet, he built up enough speed, flew off the bow of the ship and disappeared. We immediately saw a spray of water come back up over the bow of the ship. My buddy next to me said, "He's running underwater!" Well, you knew that was not true because all you had to do is just touch the water with the prop and it would wind it into a pretzel. Then, all of a sudden, the plane came struggling up into the air. The fellows by the catapult controls could see the whole thing over the side. They said, the plane came down and the pilot folded gear as soon as he left the deck (probably all in one motion). A wave hit the belly of the plane with the propeller ahead of the wave and threw up spray and put him into the air.

One of my best friends by the name of Duffy was working the barrier area while we were landing planes. This was a critical area because it kept the landing aircraft away from the fueling and bomb loading areas and could save a plane if the barrier was folded at just the right moment. About once a week, Duffy, would save an airplane by folding his barrier down. If we were not in a critical landing position, the Signal Officer would wave the landing planes around for another pass. Duffy would take off his helmet, goggles and gloves and stand up on the waterway with his hands clasped together over his head and everyone on the flight deck would give a great big cheer for Duffy. Then he would put his helmet, goggles and gloves back on, and wave back up to the Air Officer. The green flag went up, the red flag out and we were landing planes again.

The pilots were always real anxious to get back into the air. They all wanted to go home Aces. If their planes were damaged, the pilots would pace the deck. A pilot from one of the planes Duffy saved came into the catapult shack one day while we were sitting around telling stories and wanted to thank Duffy for saving his plane. He began asking us where we were all from, he was from the Midwest somewhere, and I told him I was from the State of

Washington. "Washington!" he said, and was immediately mad. I asked what was wrong with Washington. He said, "Those people in Washington...What a bunch of no good people they are!" I asked him why he felt that way, and he said he was flying a plane from San Diego, California to Sand Point, Washington, when he got into fog. He was diverted to Portland, too much fog. Then to Tillamook, too much fog. By this time, he was running low on fuel and had to bail out to avoid the mountains. He ended up in a tree along side Highway 99 (which is now I-5). He hung by his parachute harness in a fir tree, thirty-feet in the air. The motorists, who saw him, stopped their cars, took out their cameras and took pictures! He hollered to them, "Call the Police! Call the Highway Patrol! Call the Navy! Call Somebody!" More cars stopped, he gave them the same message, and the cars drove off. By this time his legs were going to sleep, his parachute started to tear through the branches, and he fell into the soft brush below. He was unhurt, but I could understand why he was so grumpy about people from Washington.

Aboard the Saratoga we had our favorite and least favorite planes to work with. The TBF Torpedo Bomber and the F6F fighter were our favorites because they were almost indestructible. I've seen them come in for a high landing, hit hard and even blow the wheels and the next day be flying again. On the other hand, the Corsairs were weak airplanes. They were good in the air, but if they hit too hard, they could put the tail wheel up through the rudder or break the engine right off in front of the cockpit. It would always end up with a fire. Although, I did see a Corsair make a water landing one day. It came around the down wind leg and ran out of fuel. The water was very rough with lots of whitecaps. The airplane hit the first whitecap and you saw the wings a flying, the next white cap the engines flying. The escort was

251

able to pick up the pilot unhurt, so I believe the Corsair cockpit was reinforced well.

Our least favorite was the SB2C Curtis Helldiver. More than half of these planes we had on deck at any given time were red tagged with some problem or other.

On the Saratoga we had two tracks of Hydraulic/ Pneumatic catapults. The track was 76-feet long, but speed was accomplished in 9-feet and the rest was carried through, the shuttle slowed down and dropped the cable. The G-force was so great getting from zero to 90-mph in 9-feet that if the pilot did not have his head back against the headrest on launch, it would tear the helmet right off his head. The Corsairs had the great big Mixmaster props and therefore had terrible torque. They had to take off at almost full rudder to compensate. They would leave the deck, turn starboard, get their prop wash off the deck and then straighten out and climb for altitude. However, one day, three Corsairs in a row left the deck, did a right hand half roll and crashed into the ocean. As the ship passed the crashed planes, we could see the pilots slumped over in the harness. They probably hit their heads on the gun sight or something, so when they hit the water, depending on how much fuel they had aboard; down they would go. A real tragic loss. I had the idea that the cause of this problem could have been the map boards, which were located under the instrument panel in the cockpit. They were built on tracks that could slide in and out and had catches to secure them when not in use. I remembered noticing at times, as I was parking the planes, that the pilot would often forget to latch their map board. Consequently, on launch the map board could slide back, hit the stick, and because they were full rudder, with all that G-force, probably could not recover. With the stick thrust back and with full rudder, they were just ripe for a roll.

I enjoyed my time on the Saratoga. After V-J Day, as we were getting the ship ready for the atomic test, we celebrated its 19th birthday. I thought that was great because I was also 19. In its career, 98,549 landings were made. One particular day, we landed a total of 643 planes. That was without anyone rushing. We started out at daybreak and took it easy. Really, we could have crowded in another hundred landings or so. The count from that day stood as a fleet record for at least WWII. We had a Commander come aboard the last few weeks of the war. He was going to make the 100,000th landing. Thankfully, he didn't have to because we had V - J Day, and it was all over."

Today Mr. Ross enjoys his charter boat off the Kona Coast in Hawaii

JOHN SAVONA

Branch of Service:
    U.S. Marine Corps (Sergeant)
Years of Service:
    1948 - 1952
Outfit:
    Weapons Company, 1st Battalion, 1st Regiment,
      1st Marine Division
      (Colonel Chesty Puller - Regimental Commander)
Areas Stationed:
    Korea
Specialty:
    Ammo Sergeant for 81mm Mortars

"During the Battle of Horse Shoe Ridge, April 24, 1951, and the unending firefight that ensued, do to the collapse of the Rock Unit on our flank, our three gun emplacements were exhausting their ammo.

I personally assumed responsibility of re-supplying their weapons. Some of the ammo carriers had been wounded. I recall running back and forth and machine gun fire bursting near my feet as I attempted to zigzag my route. The gunner on one of the 81s was wounded. I assumed his position for a traverse and search of nine rounds and then was relieved by the squad leader.

At some point, near daylight, crawling back to the weapons carrier, standing to retrieve another box of ammo, I was hit on my right backside with the slug going through my right kidney and exiting the right front side.

I was assisted by J.J. Barresh, Jack King and Corpsman 'Doc' Gibson and eventually evacuated to a M.A.S.H. unit,

10-miles from the lines. Lieutenant John O'Brien recommended me for the Letter of Commendation. J.J. Barresh received a hit in one of his shoulders as he was helping to carry me away on a stretcher."

Mr. Savona earned the Purple Heart, Letter of Commendation, Unit Citation, Korean Combat, five Battle Stars and a Good Conduct Award.

John Savona (left) with Ed Reeves, 1990 Chosin Few reunion

LEE W. SCHAEFER

Branch of Service:
  U.S. Navy
Years of Service:
  January 1944 - May 1946 WWII
Areas Stationed:
  South Pacific
Ships:
  Light Cruiser U.S.S. Mobile (CL- 63)
    Commissioned March 24, 1943
    Decommissioned May 9, 1947
Specialty:
  Electrician (Electrician's Mate Second Class)

"I dropped out of high school in Richmond, California to join the Navy at age 17.

Our ship assisted in the bombardments of Saipan and Okinawa. We also supported the Allied landings at Leyte, Luzon, Mindanao, and Mindoro in the Philippine Islands; Eniwetok in the Marshall Islands; and Palau in the Caroline Islands.

Two weeks after the atomic bomb was dropped on Nagasaki, we arrived as a member of the 'Magic Carpet' Fleet to pick up Dutch, Australian, British, and American POWs from the Bataan Death March and deliver them to Guam. While we were there for an extended period, we saw the valley were the atomic bomb was dropped in an industrial area. Torpedoes and ammunition were manufactured there. Downtown Nagasaki was not destroyed."

WESLEY D. SCHIERMAN

Branch of Service:
   U.S. Air Force Reserve (Major)
Years of Service:
   1953-1974 Vietnam and Laos conflicts
Outfit:
   116th FIS, WA ANG; 481st TFS; 67th TFS
Areas Stationed:
   Spokane, Washington; Cannon AFB, New Mexico;
   Kadena AB, Okinawa
Aircraft:
   Tactical aircraft flown: AT-33, F-86, F-94, F-89,
   F- 100, F-105
Specialty:
   Fighter Interceptor and Fighter Pilot

   Mr. Schierman joined the Washington Air National Guard in February of 1953. In October of 1954, he entered U.S. Air Force training at Williams Air Force Base in Arizona. On February 23, 1956, he earned his Wings and received his commission. Next, he participated in Fighter Gunnery Training at 'Willie' while flying the AT-33 and F-86 aircraft. Then he returned to Washington ANG where he flew the F-94 and the F-89's.
   Mr. Schierman worked for Northwest Airlines from 1959 to 1960, as a DC-4 Co-Pilot, and at the same time continued to fly with the Guard.
   In 1962, Captain Schierman returned to active duty, flying F-100's with the 481st TFS at Cannon Air Force Base in New Mexico. In 1964, he began flying the Republic F-105 aircraft with his new group, the 67th TFS at Kaneda Air Base on

Okinawa.

In 1965, Captain Schierman participated in many escort missions in Laos and North Vietnam. On August 24, 1965, while leading a flight of four F-105's, Mr. Schierman was forced to eject from his aircraft near Son La, North Vietnam due to a gun malfunction that disabled his aircraft. He was captured and held as a POW for the next seven years. He was released on February 12, 1973.

Mr. Schierman chose to leave active duty as a Major, and then returned to Northwest airlines where he flew as a Captain on the B-727, DC-10, and B-747 aircraft. He retired from the airlines in 1995 and now enjoys flying his experimental RV-4.

HOWARD L. SCHWEND

Branch of Service:
    U.S. Marine Corps
Years of Service:
    1961 - 1966 Vietnam
        Entered as Second Lieutenant, September 1961
        Discharged as Captain, July 1966
Outfit:
    3rd Battalion, 3rd Marines
Areas Stationed:
    Chu Lai, DaNang, South Vietnam
Aircraft:
    H-34
Specialty:
    Aviator; Aviator Expert assigned to the Infantry
        Battalion as a Forward Air Controller (FACK)

"My job as an aviation expert included directing ordnance to support the troops and mostly working with helicopters in planning and executing troop lifts, re-supply and other operations. I also was the one to call for and direct the evacuation of wounded and KIAs. I was assigned a communication team of four to carry and use the three radios assigned to the 'FACK' team. We were very busy as we were farmed out to the Vietnamese Army and Marine units if we were not used by the U.S. Marines.

My experiences were quite varied as I was in Vietnam early in the conflict and many of the tactics and procedures had to be incorporated during the first times and as unforeseen problems arose. I seemed to be in the middle of every battle and action that took place in 1965. Operation

Starlight was the first large scale battle of the U.S. unit and
N.V.A. unit. It was also the first in history of a large multi-
battalion helicopter lift of troops into battle for the USMC.
It was a very active and memorable few days for my team in
the middle of the battles. We experienced about everything
from joy to terror.

My experiences in the military were a test of my character
and my integrity and I learned about brotherly love amongst
combat veterans. It was a maturing process for me that I am
thankful for to this day. Even though I sensed
disappointment and was saddened by the reception the
Vietnam vets received for our service, I am still to this day a
patriotic and appreciative American, loyal to my country and
my fellow servants. I still believe in the cause in SE Asia,
and agonize over the similarities and mistakes of then and
now. I certainly never want the country to lose it's resolve
again, and welcome home it's warriors (as my comrades
were not) welcomed home from Vietnam. 'Welcome Home'
are beautiful words, even now.

I have attended reunions for the helicopter and infantry
units that I served with during that era. It was great to
reconnect to several that I have had a unique experience to
share in a unique relationship. I was reminded again of how
blessed my life has been and how dear my military
experiences are to my soul. We got little confirmation upon
our return so the mutual confirmation we get from each
other is important."

CHARLES A. SELLENTIN

Branch of Service:
    U.S. Coast Guard (Taken over by the U.S. Navy before
    the war started)
Years of Service:
    1940 - 1945 WWII
    1950 - 1952 Korean War
Areas Stationed:
    Pearl Harbor, Hawaii; South Pacific; Korea
Ships:
    U.S.C.G. Taney, U.S.S. Glendale, U.S.S. Scott,
    U.S.S. Stickell
Specialty:
    Fireman, Machinist Mate

"At age 17, I joined the Coast Guard for a three-year hitch
and took basic training at Port Townsend, Washington. The
military was gearing up for war, and three other brand-new
sailors and I were sent to Pearl Harbor. We were sent first
class on the luxury liner Matsonia, and we had 50 cents
between us. There were two swimming pools, great food,
and we shared a stateroom. We had a ball for a week, and
we thought the military was a pretty good deal. This was
very exciting for a young farm boy who had never seen the
ocean before.
    I was assigned to the U.S. Coast Guard Taney, a 327-foot
cutter with a crew of 300 men. After getting settled on the
Taney, our first trip was to some islands in the South Pacific.
The day we went over the equator, was a big day for us
'Pollywogs'. Two days before getting to the equator, they
started torturing us by having us kiss the feet of the

'Shellbacks', saying 'Yes, Sir' and 'No, Sir' to the guys who
had crossed the equator before. They had a big tank full of
garbage and all kinds of things. I was a 3/C Fireman, they
shackled me to a Seaman, and we had to go around that way
all day. He stood my watch, and I in turn had to stand his
watch. When we went across the equator, guys were hitting
us with big paddles and making us go into the sloppy tank.
That all took place before the war and they do not do that
bad thing anymore. They just issue guys a deep-sea
certificate and then they are a 'Shellback'.

After crossing the equator, we went to Howland Island
looking for Amelia Earhart, or the remains of her plane. She
had crashed in 1937, near Howland Island, trying to be the
first woman to fly around the world. Many rumors were
circulating that perhaps she had been captured by the
Japanese, etc. We also went to Samoa, Tahiti and other
interesting places. It was quite a trip for a 17-year old farm
boy.

The Navy took over our Coast Guard ship and painted it
battleship gray in early 1941. We were refitted to serve as a
destroyer, and then Pearl Harbor's Coast Guard crews were
under the command of the Navy. Hawaii was the most
beautiful place I had ever seen and everything was new to a
farm boy. Navy food was really something, and I had never
seen guavas, avocados or artichokes before. My first job was
in the galley where I scrubbed pots and pans. All new sailors
had to start at the bottom and work their way up, so I
worked in the galley for three months before being
promoted to the engine room as assistant fireman. I was the
youngest man on the ship, but I got along well with the other
sailors. We were responsible for maintaining and taking
care of the oil-fueled steam turbines that powered the ship.
We worked four hours on, and eight hours off, around the

clock. We always had hot coffee, and we had a hot plate where we cooked things like bacon and eggs. The engine room had many visitors. We new sailors had to sleep in hammocks during the off hours, and we had to work our way up to being assigned a bunk.

I liked my military assignment, and like all Americans, I was completely surprised by the Japanese attack on the morning of December 7, 1941. We were anchored next to the Pearl Harbor power plant at Pier 7 with the engines down and most of the crew off duty. I was looking forward to a laidback Sunday afternoon below decks in the Taney's engine room. That all changed in an instant. I heard the alarm go off, ran up the ladder and everything seemed to take off in a blast. The attackers were trying to sink the big battleships. A dive-bomber flew overhead, it seemed almost close enough to touch, and our 5-inch guns fired at the plane. The concussions broke all the windows of the Pier 7 warehouse next to us and showered glass all over our ship. Overhead there were bombers and fighter planes going over, and for a moment, most of us were just spellbound. We had no idea who was attacking us. I ran to my battle station under the bridge, and then we got orders to bring up the steam so we could move the ship. I couldn't see anything from where we were, but two miles away on battleship row, there was a huge cloud of smoke, continuous explosions and noise.

About an hour later when there was enough steam to propel the ship, the Taney left the dock and headed toward the mouth of the harbor to patrol for enemy submarines. Pearl Harbor had a metal mesh gate across the entrance, which was designed to keep submarines out. However, the gate had to be opened to let ships in, and when that happened, subs might sneak in also. The Taney and another destroyer, the U.S.S. Ward performed circular maneuvers, and if a sub was sighted, we could converge on the spot and drop depth charges. The charges were 25-gallon barrels of explosives, with a timed fuse to explode at a certain depth. We got credit for sinking one sub and a partial on another.

The Taney went into the main harbor to re-supply, and then we saw the extent of the surprise attack. We saw the battleship Oklahoma turned over on its side, and the area where the battleship West Virginia had gone down. It was an awful thing to see all the destruction, oil and debris from destroyed ships floating in the water, and a lot of bodies.

The Taney guarded the gate for 15 days, and then we escorted supply ships to the South Pacific. We were in the area, but did not get involved in the Battle of Midway. We were on convoy duty after that and guarded supply ships from submarine and air attacks.

In 1942, after graduating from machinist mate school, I was transferred to the U.S.S. Glendale, (a frigate similar to the Taney), to help get it upgraded and put into action. From there I was transferred to the U.S.S. Scott, a troop transport ship. We took military personnel to the Solomon Islands, New Caledonia and the Philippines and brought back the injured and wounded. I was honorably discharged from the service in October 1945, but was recalled into the Navy in 1950, to serve in the Korean War. I served for two years on the U.S.S. Stickell.

I do not hold any grudges against the Japanese who attacked Pearl Harbor. They had their jobs to do, too. If the war had not started when it did, things could have been much worse, as the Japanese were getting stronger all the time in the Pacific. God is still in control, so if He let the attack on Pearl Harbor happen, then that's how it was supposed to be."

DOUG SIMMONS

Branch of Service:
>U.S. Air Force

Years of Service:
>10 years

Outfit:
>AACS; Troop Carrier; Search and Rescue

Areas Stationed:
>United States, Greenland (Sondestrom)

Ships or Aircraft:
>Many and various

Specialty:
>Air Traffic Control Officer
>High Altitude Flight Facility Check Pilot
>Rescue Crew Pilot

"I finished pilot training in fighter type jets and then went to Air Airways Communication Service (AACS). I was a Flight Facility Officer and commanded several GCA units, towers and air traffic control sectors. I used jet and conventional aircraft to check the operation of navigation facilities throughout the country for accuracy and readiness.

After active duty I flew with a troop carrier squadron and then on to the 304th Air and Sea Rescue Squadron."

ROBERT L. B. SMITH

Branch of Service:
> U.S. Navy

Years of Service:
> July 1961 - October 1966

Outfit:
> HS-2

Areas Stationed:
> NAS Pensacola and NAAS Ream Field
>> (borders Tijuana, Baja California)

Ships or Aircraft:
> Deployed aboard U.S.S. Hornet
> Flew SH-3A

Specialty:
> "Our squadron mission was in ASW (Anti-Submarine Warfare) to locate and track submarines. We also did utility work of anything the Navy could think of."

"My whole Navy career was a great adventure and training experience. After graduating from college, (University of Colorado), I spent almost 1 1/2 years in Pensacola, Florida going through flight training with other young men from all over the United States. I ended up in the San Diego area flying helicopters.

I made two deployments aboard the aircraft carrier U.S.S. Hornet. The first was for 6+ months to the Japan area and involved primarily training for tracking submarines. The second cruise was for about 7-8 months mostly off the Vietnam Coast in the earlier stages of the war as the bombing of the Hanoi and Haiphong Harbor was developing. I flew mostly at night, tracking small boats that

might be smuggling arms from North to South Vietnam.
Our trip home took us by many of the WWII islands down to
Sydney, Australia and then on to the United States."

FRANK "MICKEY" SNYDER

Branch of Service:
   U.S. Army
Years of Service:
   3 1/2 years
Outfit:
   Patton's 7th Armored Division
Areas Stationed:
   England to Normandy (D-Day), France, Belgium,
   Germany (Bastone)
Specialty:
   Rifleman

When Mr. Snyder signed up for the military service in
1943, he was hoping to be in the Navy or Marines. As it
turned out, the man at the recruiting station signed his
paper and told him he was in the Army.

Mr. Snyder was a rifleman on the front line from D-Day
until Germany surrendered in May of 1945. He landed
under enemy fire at Omaha Beach on D-Day. As soon as he
stepped off the landing craft, his heavy gear weighed him
down causing him to sink in the water all the way over his
head. One of his buddies pulled him to shore. As he was
fighting his way off the beach and over the bluff, he was hit
in the knee with shrapnel from an exploding German
artillery shell. The piece of metal was removed and he was
stitched up and sent back to his unit to continue fighting.

Mr. Snyder's job in the Armored Infantry was to go in
first and clear out anything that could be a threat to the
tanks. He did this for the remainder of the war.

He fought in battles at St. Lo, Aachen, and the Battle of

the Bulge. His unit blitzed through France, Belgium and Germany. He also met up with Russians at the Elbe River.

As his unit quickly moved from place to place, they passed through the concentration camp at Dachau. He saw what looked like stacked firewood, but turned out to be bodies covered with snow.

Mr. Snyder was always very kind to the children he met in Europe. He frequently gave his candy ration to the kids. When on kitchen duty, he often gave out food to the hungry children who searched for food in the American garbage cans. He would get into trouble for doing so, but kept on anyway. Once he was fined two-months pay for giving out food.

Mr. Snyder did not receive the awards he earned until 1997. A close friend of his pursued the medals for him. It took him several years and numerous letters to lawmakers and even a letter to President Clinton to help Mr. Snyder get his rightful awards. Finally, he received his four Bronze Stars for Valor, a European Campaign medal, the Combat Infantryman's Badge and the Purple Heart.

Mickey Snyder, displaying his awards

270

WILLIAM D. SPORTS

Branch of Service:
> U.S. Marine Corps (TSGT)
> U.S. Air Force

Years of Service:
> 1947 - 1970 (Korean War)

Outfit:
> Howe Company, 3rd Battalion, 7th Marines,
> 1st Marine Division

Areas Stationed:
> China, Japan, Thailand, Hawaii, Guam, England,
> Germany, South Carolina, New York, California,
> Utah, Colorado

Ships and Aircraft:
> Ships: U.S.S. Randall, U.S.S. Mann, U.S.S. Springfield,
> U.S.S. Jefferson, U.S.S. Bexar, U.S.S. Henrico,
> U.S.N.S. Sultan, LST Q058, U.S.S. Jackson
> Aircraft: C-121, C-124, C-130

Specialty:
> (U.S.M.C.) Infantry-Machine Gunner
> (U.S.A.F.) Ammunition Forman

Guard Duty , 1948

"I joined the Marines in 1947, and went to Boot Camp at Paris Island, South Carolina. I was then sent to China via Hawaii, Guam, Iwo Jima, Okinawa and Japan aboard the U.S.S. Mann. I was in China almost two years at Tsingtao, guarding such places as Admiral Turner Joy's home off base. When we left Tsingtao in May of 1949, aboard the U.S.S. Springfield, we could hear Mao Tse-Tung's communist guns in the distance as his troops were over running all of China.

I was at Camp Pendleton, California when in 1950, we (1st Marine Division) boarded ships at San Diego for Japan, to prepare for the Inchon landing in Korea. After the landing, we went on to liberate Seoul. Then we boarded another ship in Inchon and made another landing at Wonsan, North Korea. We went up to the Chosin Reservoir where the First Marine Division was surrounded by ten Chinese Communist Army Divisions. For two weeks we fought night and day in- 40-degree cold, in a life and death struggle to stay alive. The Chinese had orders from Mao to annihilate the 1st Marine Division to the last man. They tried to do just that, but they had not fought the U.S. Marines before. We came out of there with our dead, wounded and equipment. We completely destroyed seven of the ten Chinese Divisions and the other three were so chopped up that they could not offer much resistance at all. We credit our Commander Major General Oliver P. Smith and his brilliant military tactics with getting us (the 1st Marine Division) out of that hellish trap alive, those of us who lived. Seventeen Medals of Honor were awarded for the two-week battle, more than for any single battle in American history.

Chosin Reservior area, 1950

In 1968, (U.S.A.F.) I had the privilege of being in charge of the largest ammunition depot in the U.S.A.F. at Hill Air Force Base, Utah."

RONALD L. STANDIFORD

Branch of Service:
U.S. Army
Years of Service:
1966 - 1969 Vietnam
Outfit:
196th Light Infantry Brigade, MAC-V Headquarters
Areas Stationed:
Tay Ninh and Saigon, South Vietnam
Specialty:
Infantryman

"I was 18-years old and enlisted in the Army right out of high school. After Basic and Advanced Infantry training, I was sent directly to Vietnam, about 75-miles NW of the capitol of Saigon, on the Cambodian boarder. Our mission was to keep the Viet Cong and North Vietnamese Army from entering the South, from their base camps in Cambodia. On a six-man patrol into a hostile area, we were ambushed and everyone was either killed or wounded. This was in the spring of 1967.

I spent 9-months in the hospital in Vietnam and Japan and then sent back to Fort Ord in California. After being repaired, except for bullet fragments still in my leg, I decided to return to Vietnam. This was my second trip and I worked in the main Army Headquarters in Saigon, sorting and transporting classified documents. This was considerably safer and much easier duty than being in the field directly in harm's way 24/7. A total different experience.

Era Vietnam was a difficult time for our nation. Many important lessons were learned, positive and negative. Only history will tell if the sacrifices of so many were worth the cost."

LEN STEVENS

Branch of Service:
  Royal Canadian Air Force
Years of Service:
  11/42 - 11/45 WWII
Outfit:
  426 Heavy Bomber Squadron
Areas Stationed:
  England
Aircraft:
  Handley Page Halifax Bomber
    (An aircraft capable of carrying 13,000 pounds of
    bombs)
Specialty:
  Radio Operator and Air Gunner

"After nine months of training (for Radio Operator and
Gunner) in Canada, we were shipped overseas to bases in
England. Once there, we were combined with other men for
a complete seven-man aircraft crew. These were men well
trained in their specialties: Pilot, Engineer, Navigator, Bomb
Aimer, Gunners and myself. The process of becoming a
single aircraft crew was very interesting as we came to know
others from many parts of the world. We were mixed with
men from Australia, New Zealand, England and of course,
other parts of Canada.

After a short period of flying training missions together,
we were assigned to the 426 Thunderbirds Bomber
Squadron for the 'real' thing, our bombing missions against
the enemy. We were a very lucky crew. We were able to
complete twenty-eight missions over Germany without

serious mishap.

An interesting note, the R.C.A.F. (Royal Canadian Air Force) and the R.A.F (British Air Force) flew roughly two thirds of their raids at night, while the U.S. Air Force specialized in mostly day raids. Unfortunately, no matter night or day, losses were very high for all the aircrews. As an example, a report I have read, tells of more than 75,000 Halifax missions flown during WWII, 29,000 were flown by Canadians and more then 10,000 men were killed."

DAYTON ROOSEVELT SULFRIDGE 1900-1975

Branch of Service:
    U.S. Army Air Signal Corps
Years of Service:
    1921 - 1945
Outfit:
    28th Bomb Squadron (and others)
Areas Stationed:
    Philippine Islands, Virginia, Texas, Hawaii
Aircraft:
    Jenny, Corsair, B-17, WWI De Havilland, Thomas
    Morse Pursuit Planes, Loessing Single Engines,
    Curtis, T-2 Fokker Monoplanes
Specialty:
    Master Mechanic, Aviation Mechanic, Aerial
    Machine Gunner, Pistol Expert

Mr. Sulfridge was born in Coeburn, Virginia on October 14 1900. He joined the Army Air Corps at age 21, and was shipped to the Philippines before he had any basic training. He spent several years there before returning stateside to Hampton, Virginia. In 1930, Mr. Sulfridge flew in the Chicago Air Races. Later, he was sent to Hickham Field in Hawaii and then back again to the Philippine Islands. It was at this time Pearl Harbor was attacked.

In the Philippines, Mr. Sulfridge had the opportunity to help General Mac Arthur and several other men escape from the Japanese. First, the natives took Mac Arthur to Mindanao Island, where there was a disabled plane. Mr. Sulfridge knew what was wrong with the plane, so he took the parts he needed to fix the plane, but did not take extra gas. He and his crew got the plane fixed and Mac Arthur was able to get the plane airborne. No one knew how far he would get with the little gas left in the tank, although, he did make it to Australia. (On a wing and a prayer.) Several of the men with Mac Arthur were left behind because of lack of room in the plane. The natives hid the men in the jungle. The men survived on one bowl of rice a day, rainwater, and had the constant threat of being caught. Later a rescue plane was sent back for the remaining men and delivered them safely to Australia.

Mr. Sulfridge was wounded during his time in the Philippines. He had over fifty pieces of shrapnel in his body. Much of it was never removed.

Eventually he was transferred to Texas to take his flight exam. It was there doctors discovered that he had tuberculosis and had to spend a year in the hospital. This was before penicillin and antibiotics were available. The doctors had to remove all the ribs on one side and collapse one of his lungs. He recovered and then became a wonderful stay at home Dad to his two daughters. He taught them many useful skills such as how to change tires, hang screen doors, cook, clean and how to fly kites.

GEORGE SWEENEY

Branch of Service:
    U.S. Navy
Years of Service:
    1940 - 1946 WWII
    1951 - 1957   Korean War
Areas Stationed:
    Londonderry, Northern Island, Iceland, Brazil, Turkey,
    Gibraltar, Trinidad, Panama, Casa Blanca, Africa,
    Egypt, Syria and Wake Island
Ships:
    U.S.S. Nashville (light cruiser)
    U.S.S. California (battleship)
    U.S.S. Providence (light cruiser)
Specialty:
    WWII: Storekeeper
    Korean War: Photographer

Mr. Sweeney served in the U.S. Navy during WWII. One experience he remembers took place in January of 1942, not long after Pearl Harbor. He was stationed in San Diego, California with his repair unit, when they had just received their orders to report to New York to prepare to be shipped on to Ireland. They were scheduled to board the French passenger liner, Normandy, but just as they were about to board the ship, it caught fire and over-turned in the bay. They then caught an English transport ship to Ireland.

After WWII, Mr. Sweeney went to photography school for four-years and put his knowledge to work serving in the Korean War. He was a photographer and flew in a P2V patrol bomber.

He then worked for the Department of Defense and served on tankers for the Navy for twelve-years. He retired in 1983, with the rate of Chief Yeoman-Storekeeper.

Mr. Sweeney earned several campaign ribbons and medals: The Victory, American Theater Medal, American Defense Medal with one star (Combat), European Medal with two stars (Combat), and the Navy Expeditionary Ribbon-Ireland.

ADRIAN JAMES TAYLOR

Branch of Service:
>   U.S. Army   (Corporal)

Years of Service:
>   July 1953 - June 1955 (Active Duty) Korean War
>   8 years U.S. Army Reserve

Outfit:
>   470th Engineer Company

Areas Stationed:
>   Fort Ord, California; Kaiserlautern, Germany

Specialty:
>   Mechanic and Mail Clerk

Mr. Taylor was born in Clinton, Utah. On July 27, 1953, he volunteered for active duty in Ogden, Utah after a two-year deferment to assist his widowed mother who had four children still at home. He spent eight weeks at the 6th Infantry Division Special Training School in Fort Ord, California, for basic and mechanical training.

In January of 1954, he was sent to Germany and was assigned to the 470th Engineer Company. This company was attached to the 7th Army as they rebuilt Germany. Bodies were still being found in the bombed out buildings. Mr. Taylor worked on the large road building equipment.

Later, Mr. Taylor became the Company Mail Clerk, and was assigned a jeep, in a short time, he was also assigned a driver for the jeep.

As a reward for not drinking, Mr. Taylor was chosen to drive an Officer and the Company First Sergeant from their base in Kaiserlautern, Germany to Bordeaux, France. They were required to learn an escape route incase the Russians attacked Germany.

Mr. Taylor earned the National Defense Service Medal, Army Occupation Medal (Germany) and the Good Conduct Medal.

Mr. Taylor now lives in Monroe, Washington.

KENNETH IRICK TIDWELL

Branch of Service:
    U.S. Navy
Years of Service:
    1951 - 1971
Outfit:
    VR-5 Detachment; VW-3 Detachment A; VW1-A;
    VQ-1; VF-191, O&R; VR-21; VR-3; VR-22
Areas Stationed:
    NTC San Diego, California; NAS North Island,
    California; NATTC Norman, Oklahoma; NAAS
    Monterey, California; Sangley Point, Philippines; NAS
    Moffett Field, Mountain View, California; NAS
    Alameda, California; NAS Barbers Point, Hawaii;
    Tinker Air Force Base, Choctaw, Oklahoma; McGuire
    AFB, Trenton, New Jersey; NAS Point Mugu,
    California
Aircraft:
    Twin Beach SNB, PBY, P4M-Q, F9F-5 Panther,
    F9F-6 Cougar, FJ-3 Fury, R-60, C-118, C-130E
Specialty:
    Cargo Crew, Aircraft Mechanic, Flight Crew Member,
    Flight Mechanic, Flight Instructor, Aircraft
    Maintenance Supervisor

"I went to boot camp at the Naval Training Center in San
Diego, and then went across the bay to Naval Air Station,
North Island, California. I was assigned to be a member of
the Air Terminal Cargo Crew, loading and off loading
aircraft. At that time, the Korean War was on and there was
an overhaul, and repair facility at the station, so we shipped

out lots of aircraft parts. We unloaded the Navy aircraft R4D, R5D, R6o and even a very large seaplane called Mars, which was tied up out in the harbor.

I put in for 'A' school to learn a rate, was accepted, and transferred to the Naval Air Technical Training Center in Norman, Oklahoma, to begin aircraft mechanics school.

Next, I was sent to the Naval Auxiliary Air Station in Monterey, California. I had my first flight ever as a passenger on a Twin Beach SNB. Daily flights went out of Monterey and one day the weather closed in with a terrible fog. I was on duty that day, when I and another sailor were sent to guard five aircraft that had landed at Salinas, California. We were driven over in a Navy pickup and spent the whole night watching over those five aircraft. The next morning a Twin Beach SNB landed and five pilots got out. One pilot told us to hop aboard. I sat in the right seat in the cockpit. I liked it so much that when I got back, I asked my chief how I could get a flying job. I was then allowed to be a flight observer when the pilots were practicing instruction flying. Eventually, I went to the PBY line, which had three PBY's to maintain. It was not long before I was flying as a crewmember.

I was next sent to Sangley Point in the Philippines with the VW-3 Detachment A. We were a top-secret squadron doing electronics counter measures work. It was mandatory to have a clean record, no court-martials and never have been put on report. I was a crewmember on a P4M-1Q and flew top turret between two 50-calibur machine guns. I did 23 missions up and down the Chinese Communist Coast. We moved the whole squadron up to Iwakuna, Japan and our squadron changed to VW1-A. Finally, in June of 1955, we were commissioned as VQ-1, which is still flying today. A few months after I left VQ-1, on August 22, 1956, one of the

VQ-1, P4M-1Q aircraft was shot down off Shang Hai, China with the loss of sixteen crewmembers. I knew them all.

I then spent one-year at the Naval Air Station Moffett Field in Mountain View, California. I was in the VF-191 fighter squadron, which had F9F-5 Panthers. It was not long before the aircraft was upgraded to the F9F-6 Cougar and then again to the FJ-3 Fury. It was a lot to learn in one year.

My next duty station was at Naval Air Station O&R Alameda, California, where I spent three years on the ferry line doing overhaul and repair work.

In Barbers Point, Hawaii, I was in the transport R6D squadron. We flew the R6D and I was the flight mechanic. We made many trips to Midway Island, Wake Island, Philippines, Okinawa, Japan, Alaska, and Whidbey Island, Washington.

Three-years later, I received my orders to teach the Air Force version of the C-118. I spent a year and a half at Tinker Air Force Base in Choctaw, Oklahoma as a flight mechanic instructor.

When the C-118 was phased out, I was transferred to McGuire Air Force Base in Trenton, New Jersey. I was part of the VR-3 squadron as a flight mechanic and worked on the C-130E model aircraft. We flew all over Europe and to Vietnam.

Three-years later, I received orders to report to Naval Air Station Moffett Field again, this time I was in the VR-22 squadron. Most of our trips were to Vietnam. I also made a trip to Antarctica School in Alaska, then on to Antarctica for the real school. (46 degrees below zero...Burr!) After a year and a half, the military disbanded the Navy Squadron that was flying with the Air Force called M.A.T.S. (Military Air Transport Service).

America's True Heroes

Because of this change, I was transferred to Naval Air Station Point Mugu, California. I did not fly, but was a maintenance supervisor until I retired."

Mr. Tidwell earned many service medals: The Air Force Outstanding Unit Award, the Good Conduct Award with five stars, China Service Medal, National Defense, Antarctica Service Medal, Armed Forces Expeditionary, Vietnam Service Medal, and the Vietnam Republic Ribbon.

JACK B. TOBIEN

Branch of Service:
U.S. Navy
Years of Service:
1944 - 1947
Areas Stationed:
Pacific
Aircraft:
Destroyer Escort
Specialty:
Electronic Technician

After High School graduation, Mr. Tobien was drafted into the U.S. Navy and selected for electronic school. He took Pre-Radio classes at the Hugh Manly School in Chicago Illinois, then EEM&RM at Del Monte, California, and finally RMS at Treasure Island, San Francisco, California. Upon completion of these classes, he was sent to the South Pacific on a destroyer escort.

ADRIAN F. VALLENCOURT

Branch of Service:
  U.S. Navy
Years of Service:
  4 years WWII
Areas Stationed:
  Pacific
Ship:
  U.S.S. San Juan CL -54
Specialty:
  Gunners Mate (5-inch gun mount, section #1)

    Mr. Vallencourt went through boot camp and training at the Newport Naval Training Station on Rhode Island, in January and February of 1942. On March 2, 1942, he reported aboard the U.S.S. San Juan and was assigned as a gunners mate in a deck division.

    The San Juan was involved in many battles and shellings; Guadalcanal, Tulagi, Santa Cruz, Bougainville, Gilbert Islands, Kwajalein, Enivetok, Hollandia, Marianas and Iwo Jima. One incident on August 7, 1942, during the landing of the Marines at Tulagi, a 5-inch gun mount onboard overheated and blew up from firing too many rounds in a short period of time. Five men were killed and over a dozen were wounded.

    The U.S.S. San Juan was the first ship in Tokyo Bay after the surrender. A task force was formed to go in and get the American and British POW's out.

    Mr. Vallencourt heard the reports of the filthy conditions of the prison camps and of the terrible treatment the men received. He also saw some of the men as they were being evacuated, most sick with disease and unattended wounds. At this sight, Mr. Vallencourt became very angry and was denied permission to go ashore.

EDWARD N. WARD

Branch of Service:
 U.S. Army
Years of Service:
 April 1966 - January 1968
Outfit:
 1st Cavalry Division (Airmobile) First of the
  Seventh Cavalry
Areas Stationed:
 Fort Ord, California; Fort Polk, Louisiana; Vietnam
Aircraft:
 UH-1 'Huey' helicopters
Specialty:
 Combat Infantryman

"I was drafted into the U.S. Army in April 1966. I had basic training at Fort Ord, and then I was sent to Fort Polk, Louisiana for AIT (Advanced Infantry Training). From there I went to Vietnam. We were out in the jungle all the time looking for Viet Cong (the enemy). We flew into hot LZ's (Landing Zones), which means we were fired upon as we were landing in the helicopters. We got off the choppers firing our weapons, usually M-16's. I saw many buddies shot, some killed and some wounded. I was wounded on April 4, 1967. I spent a long time in the hospital."

BRETT M. WENZLICK

Branch of Service:
U.S. Air Force
Years of Service:
1981 - 1987
Outfit:
343rd Civil Engineering Squadron
Areas Stationed:
Bergstrom Air Force Base, Austin, Texas; Fort
Leonardwood, Missouri; Eielson Air Force Base,
Fairbanks, Alaska
Specialty:
Heavy Equipment Operator

"I left Everett, Washington on December 1, 1981, for boot camp in San Antonio, Texas. It actually snowed in Texas that winter, something they do not see often. They treated us well because we had to be there during Christmas and New Years.

In January, I received orders to report to Fort Leonardwood for heavy Equipment Operating School. The mud was so deep on the bulldozer training ground that you could sink up to your knees. We were constantly getting bulldozers stuck. We Air Force recruits trained for three months with the Army and Marine trainees. I remember the Marines were a close bunch of young men who stood together well, and their marching songs were among the best.

In May 1982, I got my first assignment, which was one year at Bergstrom Air Force Base in Austin, Texas. It was sunny, hot and nice just about every day. The only regret I have is that I did not stay in Austin longer. I learned to operate the airfield sweeper and cleaned the streets, parking lots, and aircraft landing areas. When it was time to dump the sweeper's dirt box, called a 'Hopper,' I had to make sure to stand to the side incase a snake or scorpion was sucked up along with the dirt. Being sucked up would not necessarily kill the vermin.

My next assignment was at Eielson Air Force Base in Fairbanks, Alaska. I drove the whole way with a short stop in Everett, Washington for a small vacation. Going to Alaska was a dream come true. I probably would not have had the opportunity if it were not for the Air Force.

One of my assignments took place at Fort Greely, Alaska in the city of Delta Junction. I was assigned to a four-man team to test the Trinium airfield lights for portability and durability in extreme cold weather. The lights could be illuminated for ten to fifteen years with the radioactive chemical named Trinium. We had to be very careful not to break open the sealed containers as we set them up on the airfield. When it was dark, we went for a helicopter ride to see if the lights were visible from the air. Sure enough, we could see the lights well enough to land. I was told by the Trinium contractor that prior to our testing; the lights were used by our military when they rescued medical students from the insurgents on the island of Grenada.

I enjoyed the Air Force and would recommend the military to anyone looking for excitement and change in their life."

WINFRED B. WESTON

Branch of Service:
    U.S. Navy
Years of Service:
    1944 - 1946 WWII
Areas Stationed:
    Iwo Jima and Okinawa
Ships:
    U.S.S. Putman DD757 (Destroyer)
        Flagship of the 66th Squadron
Specialty:
    Acting and 3rd Class Bolsnmate

   Mr. Weston served on the U.S.S. Putman during the Invasion of Iwo Jima. The U.S.S. Putman supported the Occupational Force and helped rescue 114 survivors of the U.S.S. Twigg after it was bombarded at Okinawa.
   One of Mr. Weston's fond memories was when he had th opportunity to "pipe" Admiral Chester W. Nimitz and the Secretary of Navy, James Forrestal, aboard the U.S.S. Putman at Iwo Jima.

BILL WILLIAMS

Branch of Service:
    U.S. Army Air Corp
Years of Service:
    One year in service
Outfit:
    8th Air Force, 388th Bomb Group
        ("H" on the tail of the plane)
Areas Stationed:
    Thetford, England
Aircraft:
    B-17 Flying Fortress
Specialty:
    Top Turret Gunner

Mr. Williams flew in the B-17 (Bugs Bunny) as the Top Turret Gunner. During his 5th mission over Germany, Mr. Williams was killed in the Top Turret by enemy fire. The plane made it back to England after the bombing mission.

Mr. Williams left behind his wife and one child in Upper New York State.

WAYNE EDWARD WOLLARD

Branch of Service:
    U.S. Navy (Aviation)
Years of Service:
    1961 - 1966 Vietnam
Outfit:
    HS-2 (Helicopter Anti-submarine Squadron Two)
Areas Stationed:
    Gulf of Tonkin
Ships and Aircraft:
    U.S.S. Hornet (VS-12)
    T-34, T-28, SNB(C-18), H-13, H-34, SH3A
Specialty:
    Naval Aviator (pilot)

"Our primary job was to fly search and rescue over the Gulf of Tonkin and North Vietnam to rescue downed airmen. I did some rescues and received three Sikorsky Winged 'S' for saving another pilots life while flying a Sikorsky helicopter. I also received Squadron Commendations for hovering over a destroyer at night in the fog and airlifting a seaman in serious condition to the carrier. I was the squadron head test pilot and spent a lot of time flying test flights where I had numerous engine failures. After the Navy I flew 33-years for United Airlines."

MILTON A. WOODS

Branch of Service:
    Merchant Marine
    U.S. Army (Corporal S-3)
Years of Service:
    Merchant Marine: 1944 - 1953 and 1955 - 1957
    U.S. Army: 1953 - 1955
Areas Stationed:
    Merchant Marine: Pacific and Europe
    U.S. Army: West Germany
Ships:
    Merchant Marine: S.S. William Buchanan and
        U.S.N.S. General Sultan
Specialty:
    Merchant Marine: Engine Room Wiper and 3rd
        Engineer
    U.S. Army: Corporal S-3

Germany, 1952

"In September of 1944, I celebrated my 16th birthday and since 17-years were minimum for the U.S. Navy, I joined the Merchant Marine, dropping out of school to do so.

My first ship was the S.S. William Buchanan, a Liberty Ship. We had a U.S. Navy gun-crew, 3-inch gun forward and 5-inch gun aft, with as I recall, six each 20mm guns. I was a Wiper in the engine room, and a 'Loader' on a 20mm gun.

My first trip was to Okinawa for the invasion. Except for target practice at Eniwetok, we never fired. In Naha, Okinawa, we had 108 air raids in 28 days. The harbor was covered by smoke to hide the anchored ships. We on the ships could not see upwards, however, pilots later told me they could see the kingposts and superstructures of the ships above the layer of smoke allowing incoming Kamikazes to locate our ships. The 'Brown Victory' a Merchant vessel near us was hit in the stern by a Japanese airplane, but that was the only hit near our ship. At age 16, I felt invulnerable, so I did not feel in danger. We were at li Shima Island when Ernie Pyle was killed, and since he was such a famous writer, all of us felt great sorrow.

During the Korean War, I continued to sail in the Merchant Marine as a 3rd Engineer aboard the U.S.N.S. General Sultan, a troop transport. We evacuated our troops from Hung Nam when the Chinese entered the conflict... Very miserable days.

Then I was drafted into the U.S. Army and served two-years of duty in Germany. I really enjoyed my time in the Army. I made Corporal and would have re-enlisted if they would have made me a Colonel, but they did not! Darn, too bad! So, I went back to the Merchant Marine until 1957."

Milton Woods and Nicholas Rider, March 2004

PAUL D. WOODWORTH

Branch of Service:
U.S. Army (SSgt)
Years of Service:
1942 - 1946 WWII
Outfit:
E Company, 187th Infantry Division
"The Angels from Hell"
Areas Stationed:
New Guinea and Luzon
Specialty:
Infantryman, Sharp Shooter, Parachutist

Paul Woodworth, 1942

The following is the WWII story of Paul D. Woodworth as told to, and written by his daughter Vanessa Verheyen, 2002 - 2003.

After nearly 60-years, the story is told of how Paul left high school during his senior year to go into the service, because his "country needed him." This was very common at that time. Many young men went into the service when their country was in great need and they had not yet finished high school.

Paul left for the Army on his birthday, February 24, 1942, just 18-years old. He left from Fossil, Oregon where he was living at the time. He traveled by Greyhound bus to Salt Lake City, Utah where he and the other new recruits got on a troop train bound for North Carolina and boot camp. He says it took seven days by train to cross the country.

After his initial basic training at Camp MacKall, North Carolina (now closed); he finished basic and then went to jump school at Fort Benning, Georgia. He was then sent to New Guinea (Between China and Australia in the Pacific theater). The company he was in was "E" Company, 187th Infantry, later to be known as "The Angels from Hell." He was an infantryman, sharp shooter and parachutist. According to Paul's story, he and his troops walked across Leyte Island three times in all. On the initial trip, there was a small accident in which he was caught up in some underbrush and vines, fell over a log, and broke his right fibula. He was hospitalized for about a month in a cast at a nearby outpost hospital. His buddies wrote him later saying they were sorry he missed all the sea rations, severe heat, humidity, and giant mosquitoes.

During the invasion of Leyte Island occupied by the

Japanese, Paul leading his platoon of men fought the enemy all day and then suddenly found themselves behind enemy lines as evening fell. The troop of eleven was cut off from the rest of their company by fierce gunfire and surrounded by the enemy. As the terrifying night wore on, the troops lead by SSgt Woodworth hid and quietly waited, planning their way out. It was nearly dawn when they were on the move again, moving inch by hard fought inch. It took all day, but they did get back to their company with all the soldiers alive. For this type of leadership and heroism, Paul received a bronze star.

From what I know of his story, the initial severe fighting in Philippines started in October of 1944. The war would not end until September 1945. While in a severe gunfight with the Japanese, Paul as a troop leader was directing his squad of troops where he says, "I was trying to point out the enemy and return fire on some snipers." A fellow soldier and buddy who was lying beside him was killed instantly from a gunshot wound to the chest. Within a few minutes, Paul's own life threatening leg injury occurred. The fateful day was February 13, 1944, in a severe battle in the jungles of Luzon.

After the severe gunshot wound to the lower leg, a soldier near him grabbed a hand full of mud and dirt and stuffed it into the leg wound, trying to stem the heavy flow of pumping blood. Yet another soldier pulled him into a nearby foxhole, took off Paul's belt, and tied it around the upper leg as a tourniquet. Within a few minutes, he was hit again in the lateral knee area, (just a flesh wound he says). Because of the shelling and gunfire being so severe, he knew no one could help him. Realizing he would bleed to death with his leg virtually blown off and hanging by 1-2 inches of flesh, he crawled and pulled himself with his hands, holding onto grasses and tree debris to a field medic about 400-yards away. A third GSW injury came from shrapnel lodging in his left lower back area while getting on the stretcher to be taken out of the line of fire by the medics.

Paul was then taken to a field hospital on a small island outside of Manila for one day, where because of the severity of the leg wounds the doctors wanted to amputate. He said, "Oh, No you're not!" (I bet it was something harsher than that). Anyway, he would not let them amputate. He could not imagine having an artificial leg knowing he loved to hunt and fish. He also did not know what type of work he could do as an amputee. He states that they patched him up, gave him some blood, and put him in a full body cast. From there they sent him to Biaka Island Hospital for 3 weeks. He received the first series of reconstruction leg surgeries to put his leg back together. That is where he received his Purple Heart award from the Army. After some time recuperating, he was shipped back to the states for more medical treatment. In all, he spent 13 months in Army hospitals recovering from his wounds.

The flight coming home to America was an emotional one. The medical transport plane he was on also carried about 15 survivors from the Bataan Death March. These guys were pretty bad off Paul says. They were half starved, severely beaten, and most of them were barely able to walk. The reports of starvation, heat exhaustion, disease and brutal treatment of POW's were horrific. The Bataan POW's endured a 55-mile walk to the Japanese prison camp. The surviving men reported that if the American and Filipino POW soldiers did not keep up, the Japanese would just shoot them. Twenty-thousand were lost on the way, and thousands more POW's lost their battle for life from starvation and disease.

Understandably, telling the story now with much emotion and tears, he says after the transport plane touched down in San Francisco, he remembers as clear as a bell to this day asking the stretcher-bearers to let him down on the ground. He wanted to touch American soil again. It was bittersweet coming home knowing he would be away from the fighting, but facing still many difficult days ahead to restore his leg and life.

From San Francisco, he was processed back into the country by the Army. Then he was sent to McCaw General Army Hospital in Walla Walla, Washington for more bone graft surgeries, thirteen or fourteen surgeries in all, involving grafting bone from the hips to the affected lower leg. He was in the hospital about 13-months in all. After that, he was given more surgeries and treatment for three more months at Madigan Army VA Hospital in Tacoma, Washington. He says after he was able, the Army would finish one surgery and they would let him go back home for about a month before returning for another surgery. He also says he spent about 2-years on crutches and had several long leg casts for months at a time after the many leg surgeries.

Many years later, he would need an artificial knee due to the wear and tear on his right knee joint and misalignment of the lower leg, all the cause and effect of the leg wound.

When previewing this account his only comment was, "There are other things you don't know about, things I've never told." Even at age 82, it is clear he did not intend to tell them now.

Paul Woodworth

STEVEN WAYNE ZOLLMAN

Branch of Service:
U.S. Army
Years of Service:
2-years, 7-months, 12-days
1-year in Vietnam
Outfit:
185th Maintenance Battalion
Areas Stationed:
Hunau, Germany; Long Binh, South Vietnam
Specialty:
Heavy Equipment Maintenance
Small Arms Repairman

Steven Zollman (middle) with buddies at Aberdeen Proving
Grounds in Aberdeen, Maryland, 1968.

"I enlisted in the U.S. Army on November 9, 1967. I was
inducted into the Army in Boise, Idaho. I went from Boise
directly to Fort Lewis, Washington for basic training. I

chose to be in heavy equipment maintenance. I went to Aberdeen Proving Grounds in Aberdeen, Maryland for training in 1968, and then on to Hunau, Germany (near Frankfort) to work on Duce and a half trucks. While in Germany, I went to Garmisch for more maintenance schooling. In June of 1969, I was sent to South Vietnam. I was assigned to the 185th Maintenance Battalion, 135th Light Maintenance Company.

I was in Long Binh, which is just north of Saigon. At the time, there was a shortage of small arms repairmen, so I was assigned to work on the small arms. I spent time at the firebase near Quan Loie, which was a helicopter base that transported supplies into Cambodia. I would take a bag full of arms repair parts by helicopter, out to the recons. These recons consisted of a tank or two and several personal carriers. The recon vehicles formed a circle at night and went on maneuvers during the day.

During the time I was in Vietnam, I earned the National Defense Service Medal, Vietnam Service Medal, and the Vietnam Campaign Medal. I received an honorable discharge in June of 1970.

I returned to Wallowa County in June of 1970. In June of 1971, I married Joyce Cook and lived in Pendleton, Oregon for seven years. I worked for the Pendleton Grain Growers in their parts department. We moved back to Enterprise, Oregon in 1978, at which time I started working for the Wallowa County Grain Growers in their parts and hardware department. I have worked there for 28-years. We are members of the First Baptist Church in Enterprise and feel blessed to have raised our children in the church family. We have four grown children: Amy, Wilmer, Ryan and Brent. We are the proud grandparents to four little girls: Kylie, Rylie, Mataya and Hope."

About the Author

Nicholas Rider is 13-years old and is homeschooled. He enjoys reading WWII history, building model airplanes, stamp collecting, and spends hours listening to big band music. His summers are spent boating in the San Juan Islands and Canada.

As a member of the Civil Air Patrol, he is working towards his pilot's license. His dream is to one-day restore a WWII era airplane.

TO ORDER: WRITE

Nicholas Rider
P.O. Box 488
Monroe, Washington 98272

$20/Book - Plus $3 S/H
Checks or Money Order made out to:
Island Time Publishing